The Emotional Infrastructure of Places

To Marvin,
Lovs Your City!

PETER KAGEYAMA

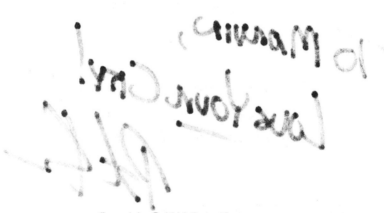

ISBN: 9781073092581

DEDICATION

To those that love, in all things.

Oh, sing your song
Let your song be sung
If you listen you can hear the silence say
"When you think you're done
You've just begun"

Love is bigger than anything in its way
Love is bigger than anything in its way
Love is bigger than anything in its way

U2 – Love Is Bigger Than Anything in Its Way

CONTENTS

ACKNOWLEDGMENTS

This is my third book and what I have learned from the process of giving birth to this one and the previous two, is that each one is a unique journey. One would believe that each successive attempt becomes easier because we become familiar with the process and, in theory, better at it. I would like to think that I have become better at the practice of writing, though you gentle reader, are the ultimate arbiter of that fact.

The journey of this book is deeply personal in that it overlaps significant endings and beginnings. The emotional rollercoaster resulting from that process actually informs this work, and I believe makes for a deeper, more mature understanding of the importance and the transcendent power of love in our lives, in our work and in our places. In the end, I can only be grateful for the all the gifts, bitter and sweet, that love has given me. Today I find myself more open, more positive and more determined to sing this message to anyone who will listen. Thank you all for joining me on this journey.

Special thanks to: Charles Landry, my mentor and role model, Rebecca Ryan, my friend and fellow traveler, Michelle Bauer for all the years, Tracey Rudduck-Gudsell for her strength and compassion for others when the world is falling down around her; truly an angel. Greg Burris, Darin Atteberry, Peggy Merris, the amazing ICMA Athenians, Phil Green, Euan Robertson, Bob Devin Jones, Rick Kriseman, Buddy Dyer, Bill Given, David Baker, Rob Karlinsey, Jim Keene, Charlie Bush, Kate & Dave Rahman, Juhi Kore, Dave Bloch and my brother in all but blood, Ken Walker.

Thank you to Michelle Royal – all I can say to you is "Wub."

And finally a very special thank you to Lisa Wannemacher for getting me across the finish line and literally carrying me when I could not carry myself.

INTRODUCTION

In my book, *Love Where You Live*, I recounted a story of a hot and stormy Florida day in August 2009, when there was a lightning strike in Orlando, Florida. No one was hurt but there was damage. The lightning struck the venerable fountain in the center of Lake Eola in downtown Orlando. The fountain was originally installed in 1912 and updated in the 1950's to include lights. The lightning strike fried the electrical system and city engineers estimated several hundred thousand dollars just to fix the aging structure. Orlando Mayor Buddy Dyer took the bold position to not only repair the iconic structure, but improve it. The proposed budget was $2.3 million. This was particularly bold given that Orlando, like most US cities at the time, was in the throes of the worst economic downturn in a generation. In fact, Orlando had been forced to cut some $62 million from its budget, which included many layoffs. On July 11, 2011 the fountain was re-opened to much fanfare and celebration. People declared that light was back on in the heart of their downtown and it seemed that the cost was quickly forgotten as people realized the value of having this iconic "love note" working again.

In *Love Where You Live*, I highlighted this as an example of the importance of fixing the "holes in the fabric of your community." The idea there is that these visible gaps or failures exact a larger toll on the psyche of your community. When the fountain is broken, people feel bad about their city. When the downtown development project stalls and you end up with a big hole in the heart of your city, people think things can't get done. Fixing these holes, I opined, does more than repair the broken element, it repairs our love and belief in our cities. I stand by all of this. Yet a few years beyond that original writing, I am now seeing the fountain, and other similar projects in a new light. This new light leads me to believe that these types of projects, the thinking/feeling behind them and their intended—and sometimes unintended—effects are evidence of another significant dimension to our thinking and practice of placemaking.

When Mayor Dyer committed to restoring and improving the fountain, despite logic and financial arguments against it, he was making an emotional decision. He must have

The Emotional Infrastructure of Places

astutely realized that there was value beyond the purely financial accounting of the project to his community. In the midst of challenging economic times, he correctly realized that it was more important that his citizens felt something positive about their city when they came to its downtown, its "psychic center" if you will. Most of the time cities make decisions that focus on the health and safety of their citizens. We expect that. We don't expect them to be thinking about our feelings. Yet, the trying times made the Mayor choose to do something that addressed the emotional wellbeing of his citizens, and also addressing some deeper issues including the actual mental health of his citizens and the overall resiliency of the community.

It turned out to be a great success and as we shall see, a highly prescient move.

Today the Lake Eola area has rebounded and is one of the hottest and most desirable neighborhoods in all of Orlando. It is also the very definition of a great place and a psychic center of the community.

I now realize that Mayor Dyer was not just fixing a hole in the fabric of his community. He was building (rebuilding actually) emotional infrastructure. What did the people of Orlando need in order to feel better and more positive about themselves and their city? He realized that $2.3 million to renovate the fountain was a bargain to achieve that goal, and a perfect opportunity to address the emotional state of his city: iconic landmark, highly visible and in the heart of downtown and at a time of economic uncertainty for the city and the citizens alike. He led with an emotional goal because the circumstances required it. Sadly, we rarely approach projects with this emotional end-state in mind. When times are "normal" we default back to the usual considerations—health, safety, financial return. These are of course valid and important considerations. No one wants to see a beautiful fountain that is not safe for kids to play in!

As city builders, we are very smart about our design of communities. We have expertly engineered cities to allow for traffic flow, garbage pick up, electrical utilities, and sewers. We have successfully added elements of great design to them; architecture, parks, playgrounds and public art—though I still believe we incorporate these elements far too late in the process of city building. Beauty, art, and great design should not be tacked on to the end of a project as an afterthought. I am encouraged by the fact that these elements are no longer considered just 'nice to have,' but increasingly seen as 'must haves.' We have come a long way in our conversation about placemaking. And I believe that our next steps in placemaking will be to embrace and incorporate emotional awareness, emotional design, and emotional infrastructure into building our cities.

What would it look like if we started with what we wanted people to *feel* in our cities? Maybe "started" is even too ambitious. What would it look like if we were at least consciously including emotional city building into our practice of placemaking? I believe we would get more projects like the Lake Eola fountain. We would get more projects that would make people feel something about their cities. This may be a conscious or even unconscious feeling about their place. Most citizens cannot articulate the technical realities of their places. Asked about their cities, they will say parking is a pain the ass, that there are too many potholes, and that the rents are too high. These are the daily realities we all deal with. Yet there is an emotional story behind each of those complaints and we are not addressing those feelings. We end up solving technical problems without addressing the underlying emotional context of those problems. We may stumble upon a technical solution that addresses an emotional need, but we are far more likely to solve these more complex problems if we are at least thinking about them in a multi-dimensional way.

I have called this book "The Emotional Infrastructure of Places" for a reason. While I am known (very happily actually) as the "City Love" guy, I speak not just about cities and towns, but a multitude of communities. When we talk about cities, we are often not talking about whole cities, but about places. Cities are wide ranging, legal, geographic, political, and demographic constructs. While we all use the term city, what we almost always mean is a place. We cannot know or appreciate the totality of a city, but we know and love or hate places within that construct. Thinking of it this way, placemaking is not just being done at the highest municipal levels, placemaking is happening street by street, neighborhood by neighborhood, and even house to house. Infrastructure is so much more than roads, bridges, airports, and schools. Infrastructure is all the foundational elements for common and shared purpose. Infrastructure is literally all around us, like the background music we can easily take for granted. It is both big and small, obvious and subtle – and it needs to considered in a different way.

Some will look at a bridge and say "It's just a bridge," and I understand the notion of not wanting to over think something. But here's the thing - infrastructure tends to last a long time, and over that time, its emergent qualities manifest, for good or ill—and sometimes both. Anything that we will be in proximity to, interact with, and are in a relationship with, needs to be considered through a more holistic and multifaceted lens. That is a high bar and a potentially confusing one; one we may not always clear. But as long as we are thinking about these issues, we will get better at consistently delivering infrastructure that solves its primary goals, does not create additional problems, and may even solve some unlikely challenges along the way.

This book is about making the case to add emotional design and intent to the process of our placemaking and develop emotional infrastructure as an overall framework for our places. What surprises me is that I have been talking and writing about the importance of emotions and falling in love with our places for years now. Yet, I too have focused on the project and its result rather than working backwards from a desired result and building elements that support those projects that will in turn create that end state. I focused on the end product at the expense of the process. This book flips some of the very foundations I have laid out in the past and hopefully challenges all of us to add another, incredibly important dimension to our practice of placemaking.

Peter Kageyama

CHAPTER 1 – 21ST CENTURY INFRASTRUCTURE

Infrastructure is a hot topic for cities, states, and nations all over the world, but particularly in the United States, where years of delayed maintenance and improvements have resulted in an estimated need of $4.6 trillion in investment. [i] This lack includes the most obvious types of infrastructure: roads, bridges, dams, airports, water and electrical systems. Beyond these immediate needs, we also need to be asking ourselves about the infrastructure our cities and nations will require to be competitive in the 21st century. To be sure, the resources above need to be addressed, improved, and modernized, but beyond that there are emerging assets and systems that will be just as critical to our way of life in the next 100 years as roads and power grids.

Most conversations about 21st century infrastructure begin with our aging transportation systems. Despite talk of autonomous cars, driverless truck platoons, and Hyperloops that can take us from New York to Los Angeles in 45 minutes,[ii] the vast majority of improvements to our transportation systems will be smaller, incremental, and a lot less interesting. Such improvements may consist of on–demand bus services, integrated payment systems, and common data standards—all of which address far more immediate needs and are at the forefront of the work already being done in cities all over the world. Cities are beginning to think about such infrastructure not merely as transportation, but under the broader umbrella of "mobility." This concept is expanding the tools, the players, the users, and even the problems cities are attempting to solve. A great example of this shift comes from Columbus, Ohio.

In June of 2016, Columbus won a $50 million "Smart City" grant from the U.S. Department of Transportation and Microsoft co-founder Paul Allen's company, Vulcan, Inc. Seventy-seven cities competed for the grant, and Columbus emerged as the winner. The city's proposal included a strong push for using the transportation grant to address social equity issues such as access to educational opportunities, jobs and, most interestingly, health care.

Columbus had discovered that certain areas in the city, most notably the South Linden neighborhood, had significantly higher infant mortality rates than other parts in the city.[iii] Studies indicated that the primary factor was lack of pre-natal care, which was directly attributed to the fact that OB-GYN services were not readily available in those neighborhoods, necessitating lengthy excursions on infrequent public transportation. Because of the paucity of service in the system, expectant mothers in these poorer areas did not seek the necessary pre-natal care to which other, more affluent, mothers had ample access. Simply put, the poor, primarily African American mothers did not use the bus system because it didn't work well.

Columbus made this issue the centerpiece of its Smart City bid. By proposing to use transportation resources to lower infant mortality rates and raise the bar on social equity, they took an unusual approach to seeking such funding. Their thinking impressed the decision makers who awarded the grant to the Ohio city.

Fulfilling the promise of this idea will be challenging. Some local critics have already suggested that the effort is a guise for gentrifying the very neighborhoods it most seeks to serve.[iv] Enhancing the transportation assets and connectivity of South Linden to the broader city may trigger growth and redevelopment—and the possibility of gentrification. Time will tell, but it is nonetheless significant that Columbus is looking at infrastructure such as bus service with the added lenses of social justice, equity, environmental sensitivity and resident health.

Our 20th century infrastructure was largely built with insensitivity to such considerations. As a result, we have had to address the externalities of development in other ways. Neighborhood associations appear in response to highway systems that sought to sunder them. Public art seeks to mitigate bland, or downright ugly, buildings. Park systems become catchments and filtration systems for ground water run off from our massively paved cities. The 20th century is replete with amazing innovations and adaptations to the emergent qualities of poorly conceived infrastructure. We got very smart in how we responded to these externalities. I believe that in the 21st century, we will need to be thinking about these things as part-and-parcel of infrastructure projects, as opposed to something we bolt on at the end. Infrastructure must not only be technically correct, soundly engineered, and economically viable, it must now be environmentally sustainable, aesthetically pleasing, socially equitable, and consistent with our values.

My concern is that in the mad rush to build, fueled by

both enormous financial potential and exigent needs, we build merely to the immediate requirements and the most basic of solutions. Many will want to build quickly and, of course, make things functional and safe, but leave out the deeper opportunities of emotionally resonant projects. As I noted before, we will live with this infrastructure for a long time, and over that time its qualities emerge. My hope is that we build with multiple goals and considerations in mind. We must solve the physical, technical, and financial problems, but we must also address the emotional problems and look for opportunities to create new levels of emotional connectivity to our places. In doing so, let's open up new areas of opportunity across the spectrum of our places. Where do we begin? Being American, we start with the car, of course.

Charging Stations

In the United States today, there are more than 150,000 places to buy gas for your car.[v] This includes both traditional gas stations and convenience stores that sell gas. There are over 4 million miles of roads and highways in the U.S. [vi]

In October of 2018, the United States reached the significant milestone of one million electric vehicles (EVs) sold.[vii] Even this number represents far fewer than 1% of the total vehicles, an estimated 250 million cars and trucks, on the road in the U.S.[viii] Yet, it is a significant harbinger of things to come. According to various estimates, 60-65% of all vehicle sales in the U.S. will be EVs by 2050, but that percentage could climb higher in the event of increasing oil prices.[ix] Around the world, countries with higher petroleum costs are moving much more aggressively towards electric and hybrid vehicles. In Norway, 42% of all new cars registered are electric.[x] In July 2017, France announced that it will ban gasoline-powered cars by 2040.[xi]

The numbers are impressive. The stock market is telling. Industry leader Tesla has had a roller coaster ride. Despite slowed production and the ouster of their charismatic CEO Elon Musk, Tesla is valued on par with General Motors, a company almost 100 years older than the start-up. In fact, Tesla briefly had a market cap greater than GM in early 2017, despite GM selling 10 million cars in 2016 compared to Tesla's 76,000.[xii] The environmental argument for electric vehicles is certainly compelling (at least to some). But all those factors fail to capture the most important and perhaps the most ephemeral reason of all—the cool factor.

Once seen as technological oddities, electric vehicles and hybrids like the Toyota Prius have changed the social and cultural landscape. The Prius became a status symbol and a declaration of values despite being a pretty ugly car. (Sorry, Prius owners, but it's true. The car is the design equivalent of a pug—small, sweet and "ugly cute"). Along comes Tesla, and the electric car becomes downright sexy! The electric vehicle now has that elusive cool factor that not only declares our values but also makes gearheads and fashionistas stand up and take notice.

I recently learned a new term—or, at least, a term that was new to me. A friend of mine took me for a ride in his Tesla Model S, which has all the cool and "wow" factor you would expect. He shared the term "range anxiety," which to non-EV people may be unfamiliar. It refers to the fear of not having enough charge to reach your destination. Now, petroleum-fueled consumers would never even consider this, because there are gas stations everywhere. You would have to be traveling in some remote parts of North America to fear running out of gas. But that is not the case with EVs. The early generation vehicles had ranges under 100 miles, which made them fine for quick trips around the city but little else. Today, the latest models from Tesla, Toyota and GM have ranges over 200 miles, some over 300 miles. Yet range anxiety still exists because of the lack of an extensive and predictable charging network. This emotional response is one of the primary reasons people cite as to why they won't (yet) purchase an EV.

Tesla recently had to address another issue regarding its charging network. Until recently, free charging was a perk of purchase. (It remains so with the high-end Model S). Apparently some people who have purchased Teslas and use them for commercial purposes,[xiii] such as Uber and Lyft driving, are charging for the purpose of commercial usage. This violates the spirit, if not the actual terms, of their service agreement with Tesla, creating a growth problem. As more people adopt EVs, including many more Teslas, opportunity for abuse of the system grows too.

Most of us can recall the experience of airports a decade ago. Remember how rare it was to find an electrical outlet in the gate area or lounges? Back then, it was somewhat unusual to need an outlet. But the rapid adoption of smart phones, tablets, and other devices made outlets highly sought after. Airports responded by installing all manner of charging stations and outlets, so today it is easy to find your connection. EV charging networks are at a similar inflection point, where need is about to rapidly increase. As of June 2017, there are more than 16,000 public charging stations with over 43,000 connectors throughout the U.S.,[xiv] but these are far from evenly dispersed, leaving some areas with near-zero coverage.

Fortunately, companies including car manufacturers and consortiums are moving rapidly to implement such networks, as they see the economic potential. Volkswagen has committed to investing $2 billion in its charging network.[xv] In Europe, auto giants BMW, Daimler, Volkswagen, and Ford are working together to deploy a so-called "Level 2" charging network, which is higher-voltage and consequently imparts a much faster recharge.[xvi] Significantly higher gas prices in Europe are driving much of the activity there, with movement in North America coming at a slower, but steady pace. We have entered a new cycle in the product adoption lifecycle— beyond the early adopters, the EV is becoming a legitimate mainstream choice for consumers all over the world. Our cities will need to reflect and actively support this reality sooner than later. Those that do will be the beneficiaries of attention and market choices made by Millennials and Gen Z over the next generation. Charging stations not only make for "smart" cities, they make for emotionally considerate and comfortable cities.

Fiber

In my first book, *For the Love of Cities*, I wrote about the (then) rise of municipal wi-fi as an amenity for the mobile, tech savvy creative class. Cities all over North America dipped their toe into the internet service arena in the hopes of providing the next "must have" service for their constituents. While wi-fi was (and clearly continues to be) a must have in the 21st century, it has rapidly become ubiquitous, with unlikely players such as fast food chains, churches, and grocery stores providing it as an amenity. Smart phones have radically changed our wi-fi consumption patterns, bringing cellular carriers into the mix, and have made those carriers the pipeline of choice for a growing portion of consumers. According to the Pew Research Center, today 10% of US adults are "smart phone only" internet users, and that percentage among younger adults of age 18-29 is 17%.[xvii]

Early attempts by cities to provide wi-fi as a service were a 20th century response to a perceived need. Cities treated wi-fi and connectivity like a 21st century version of sewer pipes or electric lines. Delivery of the service was the benchmark and goal. It is not surprising that most of those municipal attempts at connectivity have largely ceased. St. Cloud, Florida, one of the very first cities to adopt municipal wi-fi, became one of the many to shutter their systems in September 2009.[xviii] Many cities still provide wi-fi, but they typically do it in targeted areas. Often, a designated technology partner provides the infrastructure and technical support. Cities realized that while they had an IT department, they were not set up to be a service provider with all the attendant requirements.

Programs such as New York City's LinkNYC are the next generation of municipal wi-fi, yet still feel like a legacy of the 20th century mentality of providing a hardware network.

Launched in 2016 by CityBridge under a franchise agreement with the city, the LinkNYC system was viewed as a successor to the payphone system. Their public street kiosks are impressive, providing not only wi-fi hotspots, but charging stations and touchscreen computer access for all manner of city information. The planned network calls for 7,500 kiosks in the five boroughs of New York (though only 1780 are active, as of March 2019[xix]). Funded by an advertising model, the system created 350 direct, full-time jobs and had a $128 million economic impact on the city in 2016.[xx] However, many problems have emerged as the city has wrestled with some unintended—but not unexpected—externalities. Issues have included the watching of pornography,[xxi] homeless encampments around the kiosks and drug deals via the phone line.[xxii] Following these early missteps, the company disabled the touchscreen browsers and updated the software, and they have seen an upsurge in usage since.[xxiii] The latest usage figures in 2019 show over 6 million unique users of the system, using over 8 terabytes of data.[xxiv]

LinkNYC and other similar projects are ambitious, but fraught with the challenge of providing the end user with a piece of hardware. In part, they are addressing the very real digital divide that exists in our cities. Not everyone can afford a smart phone or laptop. To their credit, these systems seek to address equity of access. But moving forward, should other cities consider similar projects? Data on this is mixed.

While the costs associated with smart phones over the past five years have fallen worldwide, they have actually increased in North America.[xxv] Market research suggests that cost increases are going to follow worldwide as manufacturers offer more and more features to consumers, which drives up prices.[xxvi] Despite these costs, the Pew Research Center indicates that over 77% of US residents have smart phones. [xxvii] In fact, 64% of adults making less than $30,000 per year own a smart phone and 92% own a cell phone. [xxviii]

Cities that go down the road of providing infrastructure hardware need to consider this carefully in order to convince their citizenry on the utility of this approach. Clearly, the need for free wi-fi hotspots and charging stations makes sense. Beyond that, cities need to understand the equity and access need in the poorest of communities. The simple ability to look for a job online, fill out a questionnaire or respond in a timely manner to social services make phones a lifeline to underserved communities. Yet these technology solutions also require social and cultural training of both the intended users and the cities themselves. Technology may appear politically and emotionally neutral, but it will always have effects in those realms—and cities need to be prepared for that.

Closing the digital divide requires a multi-pronged approach, and that may need to include hardware and access points for users. On a national level, the Lifeline Assistance program, better known as the "Obama Phone" project, has provided free cell phones to low income families since 2008. However, the cell phones are basic and have very limited functionality. Further, the program has been criticized for its lax auditing and perceived inflated billing by the participating wireless companies. Locally, some cities are looking to provide smart phones directly to homeless people. These low-cost devices are provided through various nonprofits and social services groups such as Community Technology Alliance (CTA) in San Jose, California. CTA, and many others like them, provide the homeless with the "digital entryway" that is a smart phone.

Consider the smart phone in the context of both physical and emotional infrastructure. To call a smart phone today a "phone" is a huge understatement. The phone aspect is perhaps its least used and least important feature. The smart phone today is a digital entryway in multiple other ways. To not have one means you are on the outside—you are literally and figuratively outside the digital community most of us broadly share. The phone is the passport, the tool and the ticket to be part of the digital community and many other physical communities. There is huge emotional benefit to being part of a community, but I believe there is an even larger negative impact in not feeling like you are part of a community. That will manifest in increasingly negative ways, which in turn affects those of us in the community. It seems unlikely that giving out cell phones could reduce crime and increase overall community satisfaction, but it feels like that is the case.

To fully appreciate and understand the significance of connectivity, I believe we need to look at it not as the 21st century version of plumbing or electricity. Consider that plumbing pipes are a carryover from Roman times. Roman plumbing was a marvel of the age and became necessary infrastructure for the entire empire and eventually the world. Today our infrastructure approaches largely feel akin to Roman plumbing.

We need to think of connectivity as more like the concept of currency. Consider the advent of currency in the Bronze Age. Representational objects, coins and markers became the conveyance of value between people. No longer were we limited by direct barter. Currency was a foundational platform that changed everything and became something that everyone uses and benefits from. Similarly, connectivity, especially high-speed connectivity, is the foundational infrastructure of the 21st century.

Chattanooga, Tennessee, is best known for its historic connection with railroads. Today, it has become known as "Gig City" for blisteringly fast internet speeds and its burgeoning technology and start-up culture. But Gig City only came about after a bitter fight with local telecom providers over the service. In 2009, the city-owned electrical utility, Electric Power Board (EPB), proposed a massive improvement to the power grid that included fiber optic connections to residential customers to provide smart monitoring and improved redundancy and service. As in many cities all over the country, extensive networks of 'dark fiber' already existed in Chattanooga. Dark fiber is the unused, inactive fiber optic cable already laid in place by the various network builders. These dark networks are immense, but what is not present is the so-called 'last mile' of connectivity to individual homes and businesses. If those connections were put in place, improvements to the power system would be massive. A side benefit of such connections would be the ability to provide gigabit connectivity to those homes via a separate service. To put that speed in perspective, the average residential broadband speed (typically via cable) is about 5 megabit (MB) per second. A gigabit connection is 200 times faster.

Most of us cannot imagine what gigabit or multigigabit speeds look like. We rarely notice internet slowdowns or latency unless our Netflix stream dips into non-HD mode (I hate that!), or if you are a gamer and you're getting destroyed in Fortnite because your connectivity is slowed. But imagine that you have been listening to music on a mono transistor radio through a single ear bud. Then someone gives you a full spectrum of music through the latest Beats headphones. Quite a difference. But I am not sure that even captures the order of magnitude difference that a 200-fold increase in bandwidth looks and feels like.

I am old enough to recall the entire adoption of the Internet. From my first 2400 baud modem and a Prodigy account, I have seen internet speeds increase dramatically. Along the way I can recall thinking, "Wow, that was fast," and even wondering what we might do with all this broadband capacity. But the fascinating thing is that we continue to grow and expand and take up as much bandwidth as we can get. I have no idea what people and businesses are going to do with a gigabit of bandwidth, but they will find ways to use it all and then ask for more. And some of those uses will be amazing, probably game-changing for our communities.

Armed with this information and seeing the potential for his city, Chattanooga's then-mayor Rob Littlefield approached the two local telecom companies with the idea that they install the last mile of fiber connectivity. He said, "'If you will install fiber, we will piggyback on that under contract and do what we need to do with our smart meters.' They said, 'We can't afford to.' I said, 'We can't afford not to.'"[xxix]

Chattanooga is a city of over 167,000 residents in a metro area of over half a million, yet the market was apparently not big enough for the telecom providers to justify the investment in infrastructure. According to Littlefield, they said no one wanted the service and that government should not be in business competition with the private sector.[xxx] Despite the opposition, the Chattanooga city council authorized EPB to take out a $169 million loan to build the network. In an attempt to prevent the city from moving forward, the telecom companies responded with negative ad campaigns and multiple lawsuits, but Littlefield and the city persevered. Chattanooga officially turned on its municipal broadband service in 2010 and was declared to have the fastest internet service in the United States.[xxxi] The dire predictions the telecoms warned against have been just the opposite. The service is profitable, and a study by the University of Tennessee at Chattanooga found that the infrastructure investment resulted in between 2800 and 5200 new jobs, and $865 million to $1.3 billion in economic and social benefits over the 2011-2016 period.[xxxii]

Chattanooga has become a case study for benefits of

municipal investment in high speed fiber, and you would think that many more cities would be clamoring to follow suit. However, a concerted effort by the telecom industry has slowed and, in some cases, outright prevented cities from moving forward. As of May 2017, only 95 U.S. communities have municipally owned FTTH (fiber to the home) networks in place.[xxxiii] More significantly, nineteen states have regulations in place that impede or outright prohibit cities from setting up similar systems.[xxxiv]

Fort Collins, Colorado, (pop. 161,000) routinely makes the lists of best cities, and its reputation is well deserved. Green, smart, walkable, bikeable—the city boasts an amazing quality of life. However, city leaders recognized that in order to maintain and even expand upon that quality, they needed continuously to improve their city. Regarding gigabit fiber, they were facing the very situation that squeezes communities all over the country. Their local service provider, Comcast, had not invested in a fiber option for the region. The city and their progressive city manager, Darin Atteberry, realized that gigabit connectivity was necessary infrastructure for the 21st century. In fact, they described it as a necessity to "future proof" their city.[xxxv] A study of the situation indicated that an investment of $120-$150 million was required to create a public utility and connect the last mile of fiber in the region. To build this, the city would need to take on significant debt. Moreover, it would require a public referendum on the project, as Colorado is one of the nineteen states that limit a city's ability to initiate such local projects.

In advance of the public vote in November 2017, established industry players invested heavily in opposition to the measure, outspending supporters of the measure by about 40 to one.[xxxvi] Print and TV ads warned of the possible expense to taxpayers and implored the city to focus on more traditional issues such as traffic, public safety, and affordable housing.

Interestingly, the local telecom, Comcast, shifted the playbook in a significant way. When Fort Collins began considering the idea of a municipal broadband initiative, it seemed to spur Comcast to fast-track a similar service. Launched in May 2017, Comcast offered 1 GB service for $159 per month (more than twice the projected price of the city's service). But their last mile connection to the majority of residential households would remain coaxial cable, which diminishes the overall speed significantly.

Despite the well-financed opposition, Fort Collins voters passed the city referendum with 57% in favor of the broadband initiative. Across the state of Colorado, nineteen other communities voted to opt out of the state requirements limiting municipal services[xxxvii] and laying the groundwork for many more communities to follow Fort Collins (and Chattanooga) into this critical arena.

In support of the Fort Collins initiative, *The Coloradoan* editorial board noted that "Fort Collins prides itself on the pursuit of being world-class."[xxxviii] This project reflected the same pride, confidence, and values. Twenty-first century infrastructure is not just about the pipes, wires, and streets of our cities. Infrastructure has always provided the framework for public policy, and social and economic development. The infrastructure of the 21st century must also be about equity and inclusion, about what we value, what we aspire to be, and what we want to love about our communities.

Some argue that cities should not be in business competition with private industries. A fair point, but the established players have proven reluctant to invest in the last mile of connectivity and have instead relied upon existing systems of coaxial cable, and even phone lines. Without the push from municipal competition, they have little incentive to invest and modernize their systems. They are also less likely to respond to the changing values of customers and their communities.

A perfect example of this comes from Boulder,

Colorado. In the area of electrical power, roughly 70% of the US market gets its service from private companies.[xxxix] The majority of publicly owned electric companies were formed nearly a century ago, yet in the past decade or so there has been a move by some cities to take up the utility system mantle. Boulder was dissatisfied with the reluctance of their incumbent provider, Xcel, to integrate more renewable sources of energy.

In 2011, more than 50% of Xcel's power plants were still using coal and only 13% renewables.[xl] Since then, Boulder residents have battled through several highly contested ballot measures to attempt to create their own utility. What I find significant about this process is that it seems as driven *by* values as by *value*. Boulder leaders believe they have a viable financial model to run a municipal utility. But this decision is also driven by the progressive, environmentally conscious values that Boulder espouses. Political pressure alone would not move the monopoly holder to meet the standards that the community set, so the community chose to act. Xcel has responded with lawsuits, failed ballot measures to repeal the utility (five as of Nov 2017), and general foot dragging.[xli]

Others argue about the potential cost to citizens and taxpayers if a municipal utility fails to generate the projected revenue. This is also a fair point, but unlike electrical power broadband is not by design a natural monopoly. A natural monopoly "is a monopoly in an industry in which high infrastructural costs and other barriers to entry relative to the size of the market give the largest supplier in an industry, often the first supplier in a market, an overwhelming advantage over potential competitors."[xlii] Utilities are the main example of natural monopolies. The enormous cost of putting in a separate water, sewage or electrical system means that consumers have little or no choice.

Natural monopolies also begat the creation of public utility commissions to provide outside oversight of them. In the case of broadband, it may be expensive to put in the necessary infrastructure, but it is not prohibitive. Opponents of these initiatives are correct to point this out as an expense. Any investment of public dollars, especially one as costly as this, needs thoughtful consideration. However, a common point I frequently make relates to the relationship between costs and value. Everything has a cost, which we typically assign in monetary terms. But things also have value beyond the purely financial and monetary. Any conversation about 21st century infrastructure, such as broadband, must consider its overall value to the community.

Connectivity is not just about cost. It is about social justice and equity. Connectivity means access to goods, services, networks, and opportunities. Citizens will no longer tolerate polluted water or toxic air. Cities have learned this over the past century, and some are still learning it. So, too, should no citizen accept slow or limited connectivity. The gap in telecom infrastructure can lead to gaps in emergency services networks, limitations on distance learning in our schools and telehealth options for our medical providers, and even lessened governmental services as more and more of our cities turn to electronic services and citizen portals as the preferred method of service delivery. Yet within even the most connected cities, studies show that the less affluent parts of town have worse cellular and data service.[xliii] Your phone literally does not work as well in the poor parts of town because of this infrastructure deficit. We no longer accept it as axiomatic that affluent neighborhoods must have the best schools, best parks and even the best maintained roads. Today, we see this type of disparity as deeply unfair and unacceptable. We need to turn our gaze towards these 21st century infrastructure elements and realize that poor connectivity is not just bad for your Netflix stream, but it is bad for you and your community. Connectivity means we are part of the process, that we are in the game, and we have a shot at making our impact in ways both big and small.

Canine Infrastructure

As much as we love our cars and our phones, there is perhaps one love that might eclipse that emotional connection. That is our deep and abiding love affair with our dogs, which has dramatically expanded in recent generations, and is necessitating a new conversation and practice around the infrastructure to support our four-footed friends.

"Whoever can solve the dogshit problem can be elected mayor of (the city), even President of the United States," said iconic San Francisco councilman Harvey Milk in the early 1970s.[xliv] Milk, best known as a champion of LGBTQ rights, initially came to prominence through the issue of dogs in the city. It was, and is, a quality of life issue for urban residents. Dogs have been living with us in our cities for centuries now, but the recent return to cities, especially downtowns, has brought to the forefront the issue of how we integrate and accommodate these creatures into our lives and our places.

I am a dog owner. Actually, let me clarify that statement—I am a 'dog parent.' I now have three lovely, sometimes crazy dogs, and no kids. I dote on the dogs, dressing them up for the appropriate holidays, taking them on play dates with other dogs, and spending a lot of money on their overall health and well-being. I am a dog parent—and there are a lot of us.

According the American Veterinary Medical Association, 36.5% of U.S. households, or over 43 million of them own dogs.[xlv] This equates to over 70 million dogs in the U.S. In Europe, the percentages are not quite as high; Germany and the U.K. top the list in terms of dog ownership. Germany has over 8.6 million dogs (roughly 10% of the population) and the U.K. has 8.5 million dogs (over 16% of the population).[xlvi] In Japan, a country that is seeing declining population growth, the number of registered pets outnumbers children by several million.[xlvii]

Consider the all-important Millennial age cohort. Their attitudes and values are becoming the defining age segment in U.S. and around the world. According to studies, 2018 was the key year that Millennial purchasing power eclipsed that of Baby Boomers and made them the most economically significant age group.[xlviii] As discussed earlier in reference to 21st century infrastructure, the importance of Millennials' tastes and preferences has forced cities to re-evaluate their thinking and practice as it relates to this group.

As we look at the Millennial cohort, the importance of dogs is even more pronounced. Surveys indicate that 44% of

Millennials see dogs as "starter children"[xlix] and perhaps even replacements for children.[l] I don't think we fully appreciate the impacts of that attitude. Cities in pursuit of Millennial residents will have to up their game around the infrastructure needed to support dog ownership.

In *For the Love of Cities,* I wrote about how dog-friendly cities are lovable cities. They benefit from the externalities of dog ownership: street level activity, green space, safety, social interaction, and increased social capital. Dogs help humanize cities and force us to interact with each other, largely to the benefit of our cities. Dog parks and green spaces have become even more valued and seen as critical elements in making choices about where to live. No longer just nice to have, these spaces are becoming 'must haves' for cities.

In my further research around this area I was struck by an extraordinary statistic: the growing number of cities where dogs outnumber children. Seattle appears to be the first U.S. city that documented this phenomenon as far back as 1997.[li] San Francisco, with statistically the fewest children of any major city in the U.S., follows suit. According to the 2010 census, San Francisco had 107,524 people under the age of 18 and over 150,000 dogs.[lii] Seattle and San Francisco are not outliers, they are bellwethers for other cities. The decline of children in major urban areas has been well-documented and discussed. What has been less discussed is the need for dog-related urban design.

How many cities have declared themselves great places for families and kids? I hear it all the time—that orientation in design and development has driven our urban design and policy decisions for generations. Consider how much of our city is designed around the idea of supporting families with children. As Millennials delay or forego traditional parenting and turn toward pets as viable lifestyle alternatives, our cities need to rethink our fundamental approach to policy and design.

Let me be absolutely clear—I am not advocating for the supremacy or prioritization of animals over children. What I am suggesting is that attitudinal and demographic shifts need to be accounted for and included in our thinking about for whom and what our cities are designed. Significantly, these additions and accommodations are far less expensive than our education systems and other child-related infrastructure.

Even those who are anti-dog benefit from the effects of dogs and dog-related infrastructure in their neighborhood. Installing more green spaces and parklets in more areas of town adds economic value to those areas. Adding a dog park to an existing green space and playground brings more citizens together, enhances neighborhood safety, and enriches the community experience for all. Even those who don't own a dog can go and sit in the dog park and watch the puppies play. Similar behavior at a playground full of kids might get you arrested!

In response to demand, more cities have opened dog parks, and expanded parks and public green space. However, we are also seeing communities and the private sector respond with new and innovative approaches that show how far we are moving beyond this standard playbook and how dogs actually can be used to help solve many other problems.

In April 2018, the Jacksonville Jaguars announced that they would be opening a dog park at their home stadium for the 2018 NFL season.[liii] The team collaborated with pet boarding and day camp Pet Paradise to provide a 2,000 square foot park complete with a doggie pool, high speed internet, and cameras so that fans can check in on their dogs during the game. If big businesses like the NFL are paying attention to the relationship we have with our dogs, many more are soon to follow.

In downtown Las Vegas, there is a dog park called the Hydrant Club. Unlike most other dog parks, this one is a private, members-only dog park that is more like a dog country club than a park. Over 15,000 square feet of both indoor and outdoor space, the park includes water features, play equipment, and just about anything your dog would like to play with. The Hydrant Club was founded in 2013 by Cathy Brooks, a Silicon Valley transplant to downtown Las Vegas. Brooks credits a meeting she had with Tony Hsieh, the visionary CEO of Zappos, for the inspiration to move to Las Vegas. Hsieh and his company have championed the Downtown Project, which has reshaped downtown Las Vegas. Zappos not only purchased and repurposed the old City Hall into its corporate headquarters, the company has taken over several other buildings as corporate housing, and actively recruited new businesses and start-up entrepreneurs into the area, including Brooks.

As many of Zappos employees moved downtown, it became evident that they needed support services including dog walking and day care. In fact, at a Zappos all-hands meeting, Brooks heard from employees that their number one request was for doggy day care downtown. Brooks realized that this was much needed and fun opportunity for her to step into this community.

Brooks told me that the Hydrant Club is just that—a club with members who form a community. The Club acts as a dog park at its most basic level, but it also offers a range of concierge services for dogs and their parent-owners, including the much-needed daycare service for working people. The Hydrant Club is Brooks' full-time job now, along with six other part-time employees. The park is open seven days a week with daycare offered Monday through Friday. Zappos CEO Tony Hseih's dog Blizzy is a member. The Club has influenced other aspects of its neighborhood: the ongoing speaker series downtown is called "Speak," and there are several Yappy Hour events in the restaurants and bars. The Hydrant Club is a valuable piece of infrastructure, just like a supermarket or a transportation node, in the jobs-business-lifestyle calculus that is modern economic development.

Seattle, Washington, already one of the most dog friendly cities in the world, saw several innovative developments in 2017. Amazon, which is headquartered in downtown Seattle, opened a 2,000 square foot dog park on its campus.[liv] Primarily for its employees, the park is also open to the public. While certainly a positive perk for happy employees, studies also show that dogs in workplaces create positive environments for creativity, collaboration and social interaction[lv]. Companies like Amazon and Zappos are not just doing this to be cool places to work. They clearly see the bottom-line benefit to the company in having a happy, satisfied, collaborative, and creative workforce.

In the summer of 2017, the Downtown Seattle Association created a series of "pop up" dog parks. The association brought in live grass and food trucks into downtown areas such as Pioneer Park on the second Sundays of June, July and August. The main objective was to further activate these downtown areas, but there was a significant secondary benefit as well. The activation of spaces directly addresses street crime, and in an indirect way, homelessness and panhandling. Active, vibrant spaces are not conducive to illicit activity, so dog parks (whether pop-up or permanent) are bulwarks against crime.[lvi] And while these parks do not directly address the challenges of homelessness in our communities, they do address its visibility.

When homeless populations congregate, many non-homeless folks get nervous and avoid those areas. This creates a cascade effect: the homeless gravitate to places where they will not be bothered, further increasing their numbers and visibility, which in turn pushes other city dwellers away. To change this dynamic, you need create more activity that provides reasons for people to come to these areas. The pop-up dog parks were exactly that type of activity. They do not address the fundamental issues of homelessness, but they do help us collectively interact with each other and see that we can all share the city together.

Again and again, we see the positive impacts on our communities by the inclusion of dogs in our design, yet I am still surprised by how many communities struggle with the idea of dog parks and pet-friendly ordinances. The "No Dogs" lobby is alive and well in many places, but its sway over communities is clearly waning. As communities make the case for dog parks based upon safety, community building, economic benefits, health benefits (both physical and emotional), productivity benefits, talent attraction and retention, and social capital, these benefits and the marginal costs to implement them should make the inclusion of dogs in our cities a no-brainer.

Projects like the Hydrant Club and pop-up dog parks are exemplars of this movement. As I travel across the country, I see how commonplace these kinds of efforts are becoming. Most are not as nice as the Hydrant Club, but the general idea is becoming standard practice for businesses, governments, and anyone involved in placemaking efforts. I believe this goes beyond the economics of making attractive, interesting spaces and is addressing a deeper, emotional, perhaps even spiritual, need.

The relationship people have with their dogs today feels manifestly different from a generation or two ago. Granted we have changed a lot, and we no doubt treat our dogs better, and with more sensitivity to their needs than we did a few decades ago. There is also a racial component to dog ownership that is changing over time as well. White households are on average about three times more likely to have a dog than African American or Hispanic households. Dog ownership is an expense, and lagging economic progress impedes on the adoption of dogs into households. I would also be remiss to not mention that dogs were used as weapons against the African American community within the lifetimes of many community members. That emotional awareness needs to be part of the conversation. Certainly, this feels different amongst the Millennial cohort, and their attitudes about dogs will be the prevailing standard for years to come.

But that progression alone does not explain the elevated, some might say privileged, position that dogs now play in our lives. The emergence of private parks for dogs, ever increasing comfort animals in airports, high-end dog hotels, restaurants that accommodate both two- and four-footed patrons—all this speaks to a greater need.

I believe that we are using our pets, specifically our dogs, as an antidote to the physical, cultural and technological environment we have created. When we built our interstate highway system, we did not overtly intend to create a car culture that isolated us, but we did. When we built gated communities and suburban homes, we did not intend to isolate ourselves from our neighbors, but we did. When we created smart phones, social media and ubiquitous, persistent connectivity, we thought we were connecting people together. In many, many ways we did—but, again, one of the unintended consequences is the isolation of being alone among many, even while physically together and technologically connected. This same technology has fueled some of our baser instincts as well. We may always have been self-centered, stimulus-seeking, and motivated by instant gratification, but our technology has empowered those motivations and taken them to unhealthy, and even dangerous, heights. In this complex environment our basic need for human connection is even more essential.

Cathy Brooks said to me, "We can utilize our dogs to help us be more human." At our best, this is certainly true. Dog ownership, dog parenting, is a responsibility. We think of something beyond ourselves. Dogs require us to get out of our house and interact with our environments. In doing so, we may see other people and, even if we only nod a greeting, we connect with other human beings. A less generous interpretation of this affinity would suggest that our dogs are merely an extension of our self-absorption and narcissism. Is it any wonder that a creature who looks at us with love and adoration, as if we are the most special person on Earth, is going to do well in our self-absorbed, selfie-taking society? Unlike a child, the dog is the perfect accessory to our modern lifestyle. Our dogs have helped fill a very real emotional gap in our modern lives.

Regardless of the ultimate motivation people have for including a dog in their lives, as city builders, as place-makers, we need to be thinking about this reality. In an immediate sense, our places need to allow for this relationship and support it. Over the longer term, we need to think about how we created this need in people and how we might improve the systems that make up our cities. I am not suggesting that we will design the dog out of our lives—absolutely not. Thousands of years of evolution have made us uniquely well-suited companions, to the betterment of both species. What our dogs actually have done is help fill the gaps in our systems and point to the issues that require our attention. In that sense, these remarkable creatures have proven again to be our best friends—friends who love us unconditionally as we are, yet whose very companionship elevates us and points to our better selves.

Peter Kageyama

CHAPTER 2 – WALK, RIDE, SCOOT & ROLL: "CARS & WHERE TO PARK"

In the introduction to this book, I pointed out that some expressions of feeling from citizens about their cities are predictable and common across the developed world. If asked about their cities, citizens everywhere will complain about parking, potholes, and traffic. Governments spend billions of dollars on transportation infrastructure every year, yet it remains one of the most emotionally fraught aspects of our cities. There is an emotional story behind each of these complaints; if we are not addressing the underlying feelings, we are only treating symptoms and not the most fundamental issues. I doubt that the problem of transportation can ever be definitively solved, but I do know that our current approaches need a new lens and a new level of understanding, beyond technical knowledge, in order to inspire us to make better progress.

Commuting

Nothing impacts our emotional and physical health as much as our daily commute. Driving is the most stressful thing we do on a daily basis, and we spend a lot of time doing it. The average American commute is 25.5 minutes[lvii] each way or 51 minutes per day—that's about 204 hours per year spent commuting. None of us likes the drive, but we seem to accommodate it and have come to accept it as part of life. But studies show that during this daily commute, a number of unhealthy reactions occur: your blood pressure spikes, your blood sugar rises, and your back experiences stress from prolonged sitting. Over time, fitness suffers, and cholesterol is shown to become higher, with attendant risk of heart disease. Risk of depression goes up, along with anxiety, which in turn affects healthy sleep patterns.[lviii] And, as if that weren't enough, commuting is socially isolating. Three-quarters of American commuters drive alone.[lix] You can see where this is going. Psychologists have called commuting the "stress that doesn't pay."[lx]

In my research for this book and others, I have gone back and tried to recover what previous city thinkers thought about in their age. Certainly, Jane Jacobs' *The Death and Life of Great American Cities* remains as relevant today as when published in 1961. I came across the following text, written by

William Whyte, one of Jacobs' contemporaries and another lion in the field of cities. Speaking about people returning to downtowns, Whyte wrote in 1958:

> *Transportation is easier too, and a lot of things are within a few minutes' walk. Wives say how nice it is now that they see more of their husbands, and not in a bad temper from commuting either. Husbands, now only minutes away from the office, are delighted with the two extra hours they now have. Commuting, many say, took too much of life, and they mention such new-found pleasures as strolling home and gloating down from the terrace at the jammed cars fighting their way back to suburbia. "I used to be one of those poor fools," said one returnee recently, twisting a lemon peep into the martini pitcher. "Now I feel ten years younger."[lxi]*

Putting aside the sexist tone and *Mad Men* imagery of Whyte's text, it says to me that even sixty years ago people were lamenting the daily commute and praising the virtues of downtowns and walking. Nonetheless, we continued to build roads and highways to the suburbs, and when the suburbs weren't far enough away, we created the exurbs and moved even further away from city centers. The long-term physical, psychological, and emotional impacts of this infrastructure became painfully evident over time.

Many have commented extensively on the ills of car culture; I won't pile on to that well-established argument. Rather, I ask us to consider how we might address this stressful, fear inducing, and much loathed aspect of our cities. Of course, the obvious answer is to "fix" any given transportation system as a whole—a huge challenge and one you can be sure is perpetually underway at various levels of government. In addition to such efforts, I would ask how we can mitigate the negative emotions around transit in oblique and novel ways that don't cost a lot of money but may still have demonstrable impacts on our overall emotional satisfaction with our places. Advances in technology, such as autonomous vehicles, will continue to change the experience of transportation, but I would encourage us not to sit back and wait for their arrival. Such changes are not a panacea, and the emotional toll is already being paid every day, even in small ways.

Potholes

Everybody hates potholes. But why? The obvious answer is that they damage our cars. We react viscerally to potholes in a way that is deeply out of proportion to their actual impact on our lives. As I argued in my first book, potholes are the hangnails or paper cuts of our civic lives— annoying, sometimes painful, but not life altering. Yet I have seen communities where political candidates have run on a platform of fixing potholes and fulfilling the most basic of civic services.

Aside from our homes, cars are typically the largest investment consumers make. According to a AAA study, car ownership, including fuel and insurance, costs approximately $9200 per year for someone driving 10,000 miles per year.[lxii] There was a time when cars symbolized freedom, and for some this is still true. However, for most of us, cars are just expensive, rapidly depreciating assets, and anything that hastens their depreciation or adds an expense (a flat tire, for example) is going to be perceived harshly. Potholes ruin tires, knock cars out of alignment, and can even harm axles and suspension. On a basic level, they damage our investment.

Dig a bit deeper and consider the emotions at play. Potholes are tiny breakdowns in the system that is my city. They are visible and physical failures in my city. Though small, they have a cumulative effect. Every time I hit one, I think, "somebody needs to fix that," and that somebody is "the city." There is an emotional toll to these tiny failures. There is also a correlation between pothole interactions and time spent in our cars. The more time I spend in my car, the more likely I am to interact with potholes and, I would venture, the more likely I am to say how much I hate them. Our time in our cars is the least happy and most stressful part of our day. Add to that condition poorly maintained roads, and an already bad situation becomes worse. Our emotional reaction to potholes is tied to our relationship with our cars, and most of us have a complicated relationship with our cars.

Among millennials, car ownership is even more complicated. Studies have shown that millennials are delaying owning a car,[lxiii] and many are purchasing them for an unusual reason: to work as drivers for ride-share services such as Uber and Lyft.[lxiv] Overall, this bodes a shift in our attitudes about cars and commutes. When mobility is a service and I summon my ride on my phone, I don't think I will care much about the maintenance of my Uber driver's car—other than being road-worthy. So, will we really still care much about potholes then? I suspect not. Has anyone ever cared if a taxicab was dented or scratched? Never.

Parking

Once you arrive at your daily destination, you face the secondary stress of having to find a place to park. Every city will say that they have a parking problem. From scarcity to cost (both too much and too little), to surface lots, to ugly parking decks—there is one constant in every city, and that is that people complain about parking. There are, of course, legitimate issues around parking. Surface lots are antithetical to vibrant downtowns because they are among the least productive uses of valuable real estate. Parking decks are a more efficient use of land, but they are generally eyesores, raise security issues, and can become campgrounds for people experiencing homelessness. Metered parking is either too expensive or too cheap, depending on who you ask. Cities can—and do—spend lots of time and resources trying to fix these incredibly complex problems because they hear over and over from their citizens about what a parking problem they have. But what problem are they really trying to solve? What are we telling our leadership about parking?

Does this sound familiar? When asked why they don't go downtown, people say "parking is a pain in the ass." We interpret that to mean there are too few spaces, the existing spaces cost too much money, and they are not located in the areas we want to be in. Yet, a systemic look at most cities will show that there are sufficient numbers of spaces, be it on the street level or in parking garages, and that their costs are determined by the desirability of the urban destination and scaled to location. Downtown Manhattan parking prices are going to be different from downtown Akron, Ohio, and we understand this differential. So, our complaints are not actually rooted in a reality. What drives this disconnect?

In my first book, *For the Love of Cities*, I wrote about my friend Chris Miller, then from Savannah, Georgia, who had astutely opined that in U.S., "we don't have a parking problem, we have a parking expectation problem." He is absolutely correct. Our car-centric mall culture has created an expectation that we can park "close" to our destination and for free. When we have to pay to park in a downtown garage that is two whole blocks away from our destination, we lament and say parking is a pain in the ass. This attitude neglects to consider that "free" parking at a mall, in contrast, has already been factored into the cost of goods and services for sale in that mall, based upon retailer rents and revenues. Furthermore, your walk from the parking lot to the interior store is likely just as far, or farther than, the lamentable downtown parking situation. Along with the distance issue, parking has gotten complicated. From the credit card systems on parking meters to the latest phone app, parking is no longer as simple as dropping a quarter into a meter. Collectively, these conditions make people reluctant, even fearful, of parking. But people will not tell you that the prospect of parking downtown makes them anxious or uncomfortable. They will tell you it is a pain, and we city makers default to thinking it is an issue of cost, quantity or location.

The Emotional Context of Parking

Consider this: Other than the rare, fleeting moment of perfect timing when you slide into the perfect parking space right in front of your destination, all our emotions around parking are negative. The anxiety of "where to park" or "how much it will cost?" The anger of feeling ripped off, or the white-hot moment when we realize we've been given a parking ticket. How about the uncertainty and frustration of not knowing how to use the parking machines or the latest app?

No one wants to admit to feeling fear and uncertainty. No one wants to appear, or think of themselves as, weak or confused. Yet I know that I don't understand how to use the parking app for downtown St. Petersburg, and I am supposedly a globe-trotting city expert! How do we suppose that the suburban dweller who does not typically come downtown might feel once they arrive and try to sort out the parking situation? This is the underlying emotional state that is not being addressed. To "fix" our parking problem, we typically would add more technology and more capacity, which addresses the symptom but does not address the issue that the system's complexity has alienated the very people it was designed to serve and makes them feel uncomfortable, anxious, and even stupid. The missing element in our approach to solving this problem is the necessity of addressing the emotional state of our citizens and taking that into account in a holistic approach to the issue.

The Three O'clock Question

In addition to the latest technology and increased capacity, solutions can be as basic as better signage or few more "downtown ambassadors," those uniformed workers who not only provide the clean and safe element needed in our cities by picking up trash and providing routine maintenance, but also proactively help folks without making them feel stupid. The Walt Disney Company has perfected the art of customer experience in their parks and hotels to the point that they have a training practice via their Disney Institute. A well-known story from Disney business lore says that the most commonly asked question by park guests is "What time is the three o'clock parade?" According to the story, Disney cast members are taught to answer that question with a smile and not to make guests feel stupid with the answer. That is good customer service, and a lesson that cities would do well to emulate. The Disney Institute, which is the company's corporate training arm, uses this question to engage with the customer on a deeper level.[lxv] They note that the question is an opportunity for the cast member to initiate a more meaningful exchange with the guest, such as pointing out where the best vantage points might be to watch the parade. Parking is a

"Three O'clock Question" for cities and an opportunity to create a positive emotional response in both citizen and visitor alike.

Free Parking

There are many who argue that what cities need, especially downtown, is more free parking. Seems logical, right? Provide more spots and make parking easy and free, and people will flock to your downtown. Some people think that moribund downtowns and their retail woes can be fixed if only there was more free parking. This is completely wrong-headed.

Downtown should be about the unique opportunities to people-watch, explore different types of stores, touch local products, eat local foods, and drink local beers. Downtown retail can't and shouldn't try to compete with big box, chain store retail. Yet, over and over again, I hear people—often the very downtown retailers themselves—say that what they really need is free parking (like the mall). Every time, I have to shake my head. Downtowns need cool stuff to see and do so that people will not even bat an eye about parking because they are so excited about the experience of coming downtown. What is needed is retail that will surprise, delight, charm, and create a sense of identity. Generic is out and local love is in.

Here is a thought for your downtown to consider: As your city becomes more successful and interest in your downtown grows, be very cautious of using that interest as an excuse to put in more parking. Adding more parking is inducing demand, actually encouraging more cars to come downtown. Those who argue that more parking is necessary to bring more people downtown believe that the only way to get people downtown is via the car. That is the fundamental habit that we need to break. As New Urbanist architect and planner Andres Duany noted, "The more walkable a place becomes, the more people want to drive to it from less lively places. An emergent tourist or day-tripper parking problem is a symptom of success and should not be the catalyst of more parking."

Aspen, Colorado, offers a brilliant, counter-intuitive example of how to improve downtown traffic and parking by limiting it. Summertime in Aspen is a peak time for seasonal visitors; the city's population swells to three times its ordinary size,[lxvi] and downtown parking is often at 100% occupancy. Long waits and lots of circling await the visitor trying to score a parking space. A typical response to this situation would be to build more parking garages, add more street parking and more surface lots. This type of induced demand would at best be a short-term fix—a temporary increase in capacity would simply be filled by more cars, and Aspen would be left with the same situation, only with more cars in their downtown.

In 2015, Aspen hired Mitch Osur as the city's parking director. Osur did not come from a government, transportation or public policy background, but rather had previously worked as a customer service specialist in the private sector. Recalling the situation during an interview, Osur explained that he and his team set out to sell a "crazy idea" to the City of Aspen. Osur proposed to raise the parking rates downtown by 50% during the summer season, with graduated pricing that made successive hours more expensive. But Osur did not stop there—he and his team brought in a partner company to run a short-range electric shuttle service. The Downtowner operates three electric vehicles that carry up to six passengers apiece. In its first month of operations in June 2016, the service provided more than 1,700 rides[lxvii].

The major piece was a "Drive Less" program that encouraged people to walk, bicycle, or take public transportation in and around Aspen. To incentivize this, Osur's department offered a choice of free bike tune-ups, free bike helmets, or free summer bus passes to people who signed up for the Drive Less program. If you signed up, you also got free access to the city's bike share program. As a result, downtown parking occupancy rates in Aspen dropped by 12% and those people who did park downtown parked for shorter periods of time, thus encouraging more turnover of visitors to the city's core.[lxviii] Significantly, sales tax revenue for downtown has increased by 20% each successive year since 2016.[lxix] Parking is more expensive but places are now available, with fewer people circling and looking for spots, thus reducing overall traffic and creating a much better downtown experience. Said Aspen Mayor Steve Skadron, "Aspen just feels like a nice place to be."[lxx] What better metric of success could there be?

The success of the Drive Less and related programs have led people to declare Aspen an example of "travel demand at its finest" and an example to other communities of how to approach parking problems in a systematic, multi-modal manner. The success of Osur's "crazy idea" should also embolden people seeking to modify driver behavior and get beyond the simplistic notion that just adding more capacity (or worse, adding more *free* capacity) is the answer to downtown parking problems.

Economists call roads and parking a "free good," or one for which its users do not pay the full cost, which in turn induces and incentivizes people to use more of the good. Because this notion of a free good is so deeply ingrained in our culture, cities have held drivers and car culture sacrosanct, and refused to demand any changes on the part of car users. Instead, we often see attempts to regulate (or over-regulate) cyclists, skateboarders, scooters, and pedestrians. To make meaningful changes in our cities, we must be willing to inconvenience the driver in the short term, while we look to build new systems and new behaviors for moving around cities.

System Re-design

The fundamental design and engineering of our cities is an attempt to segregate transit users by type and function for reasons of both efficiency and safety. However, that thinking and approach has not been as successful in either of those areas as we would have hoped. It is only by breaking down some core assumptions that we will be able to deliver more satisfying and people-centric results.

Consider how much of urban design is a response to concerns about keeping our citizens safe. Cities go to extraordinary lengths and undertake expensive precautions to try to protect citizens. Take the sidewalk—sidewalks came into broad use in 18th century Europe. England was one of the leaders of the movement with a series of parliamentary acts including the 1766 Paving & Lighting Act, which established lighting requirements and dedicated pedestrian space in the streets of London.[lxxi] Imagine a bustling 18th century London with people walking amidst a morass of horse drawn carriages and carts. The creation of the sidewalk was an accommodation for both safety and efficiency; separating pedestrians from faster moving vehicles was good for everyone. Today, we can hardly imagine a city without sidewalks. The sidewalk is a safety feature designed to reduce the danger—and our concomitant fear—of being in such close proximity to fast moving vehicles.

Consider the "bulb-out" sidewalk design that has become a staple of modern street design. This sidewalk extension is a traffic-calming device designed simultaneously to reduce the distance pedestrians must travel to cross streets and to narrow the traffic lanes for cars. This design precipitates two effects fueled by emotion: Pedestrians feel safer and more comfortable because of the increased space, and drivers feel constrained, which has the physiological effect of causing them to slow down. This aim of slowing down cars is at heart of the "Complete Streets" design philosophy. Narrower lanes, trees, landscaping, bulb-out sidewalks and bike lanes send a message that this space is not just for cars—it is a shared space. I admire the Complete Streets mindset but believe that, at its heart, it is an attempt to tweak car-oriented designs into something else. No matter how well done, such changes are mostly a block-by-block patchwork that can never really rebalance the transportation scales. To address the broader challenge, we need to consider the entire notion of car culture and look for opportunities to change not just the design of our systems, but the underlying thinking and emotions of this infrastructure. As I noted earlier, we live with infrastructure for a long time, and its emergent qualities and the impacts on us are only revealed once in place.

Room for Bikes

By far the most common and significant alternative to the car is the bicycle. I am a huge fan and proponent of bikes in cities. In fact, I noted in my first book, *For the Love of Cities*, that bike-friendliness was a key measurement of a lovable city. When we ride, we experience our city in a different way— often, one that connects us in a more physical and emotional manner. That's a good thing, but even this lovable element has complex emotional, technical, and financial considerations. For instance, an average mile of bike lane costs $130,000 to install;[lxxii] in more complex urban environments (where such lanes are needed most), the cost can be several times as much.

In *Love Where You Live*, I noted that there has been widespread backlash against bikes all over the U.S. and in many parts of the developed world. A large part of that backlash stems from the higher visibility and presence of bicycles on roads and in cities. Increasingly, drivers are sharing the road with cyclists and, like selfish children not used to sharing toys, some of them don't like it. They may feel something has been taken from them, but as the Detroit Greenways Coalition aptly noted, the addition of bike lanes and complete streets does not "diminish vehicle access but improves them for everyone's use, to save lives, and spur neighborhood growth and economic development."[lxxiii]

The Coalition was responding to an op-ed by a well-known local businessman who decried the money Detroit was spending on bike infrastructure. "There must be better uses for our tax dollars than setting up something that costs plenty and serves few people. We were the Motor City for a long time. Now it looks like we will have to change our name."[lxxiv] His comment reflects the prevalence of the misunderstanding that bike lanes serve very few people; while technically incorrect, this idea seems to have found an unfortunate emotional resonance with some.

My own hometown of St. Petersburg has done an excellent job of installing protected bike lanes, sharrows (the painted bike symbols on the pathways) and bike parking throughout downtown. We also have a successful bike share program. Yet despite all these investments, I still too many people riding their bikes on the sidewalk.

I walk all over my downtown and admit to becoming increasingly frustrated with cyclists on sidewalks. As a pedestrian, I have turned corners and almost been run over. When I began noticing ordinances in cities such as Berkeley, Palo Alto, and Fort Collins prohibiting bike riding on sidewalks, I thought it sounded like a good idea. Then I spoke with Jim Keene, the now-retired city manager from Palo Alto, about this very issue. Keene had the unique position of being city manager in Berkeley prior to moving over to Palo Alto and saw the impact of the ordinances on both cities. He told me the main driving force behind the ordinance in Berkeley was from the disabled community. For people in wheelchairs or those using a cane or a walker, having to navigate a busy sidewalk with bikes and skateboards was just too much. Palo Alto used a similar argument to pass its "dismount zones" and, under Keene's leadership, the city began to more vigorously enforce the rules.

I can see easily how a city would endorse this type of ordinance, as it accomplished the fundamental thing that transportation regulations do—segregating users by type. I assumed that bike advocates would likewise see the wisdom of this, especially if the city provided bike lanes, sharrows and similar provisions. I asked my friend Jess Mathews, a bike advocate in Columbus, Ohio, about city ordinances that prohibit cycling on the sidewalk. To my surprise, she was adamantly opposed to these types of laws.

"Most people are afraid to ride their bikes on the street," Mathews told me over lunch in downtown Columbus. She said she could not, in good conscience, tell a rider to get out into the street and deal with cars—their fear is justified. Even with bike paths, sharrows and all manner of signage, cyclists are very much second-class citizens on the road. Drivers don't pay enough attention to them, and when they do it is often with annoyance, disdain or even hostility. She told me that cities need to work on changing the behavior of drivers, an effort that must be partly based in culture change and partly in design.

Just a few weeks later, I had an enlightening moment as I walked home. Fourth Street, is a four-lane, one-way street that runs through the heart of downtown St. Petersburg. Its traffic lights are timed so that if you drive at about 40 mph, you can speed through most of downtown without stopping. On that particular day, I approached the street corner, and seeing that there were no oncoming cars, even though the light was green, I crossed the street—as I presume most city residents would do. I had not noticed a uniformed police officer standing on the opposite corner. As I approached, she handed me a postcard about pedestrian safety that explained the proper way to cross a street and the legal implications of doing what I had just done, crossing against the light. I down looked at the card and then, a bit incredulously, back up at the officer. She said the city would be cracking down on violations to promote pedestrian safety. I said to her that the problem is not the pedestrians, but rather the cars. The city had essentially designed a raceway through downtown and rather than recognize that fact, it was choosing to blame the pedestrians. She shrugged and turned away.

That incident and my conversation with Matthews changed my thinking on these issues. Blaming the cyclists and pedestrians is not the solution. We have given far too much primacy to the car, and our policy and design decisions need to address this imbalance. As long as we continue to allow the car to dominate, our investments in bike infrastructure and the like are going to fall far short of their full potential.

Changing the Car-Bike Relationship

Why is there such an impediment to changing the conversation about bikes? Jim Keene, the former Palo Alto City Manager, had a great insight. "We see riding bicycles as recreation, not as real transportation," he told me. Moving the needle on cycling and other non-automobile related transportation is a policy problem, a design challenge, and a culture shift. We can see the design improvements that the "Complete Streets" approach, bike lanes, and similar infrastructure bring to the table. But this alone has not been enough to change the culture and perception of cycling in our cities.

In early 2018, the City of Tampa, Florida, rejected an engineering study that recommended the addition of bike lanes to the well-traveled Bay to Bay Boulevard in the heart of the city. The addition of one mile of bikes lanes was fought by businesses on the route, as they feared that construction times would impact their business. Clearly, they also believed that none of their customers rode bikes. As a result, city officials suggested that other streets could be used for bike travel.

Local residents and alternative transportation advocates were dismayed by the decision. Tampa is notorious for its poor reputation in cycling and pedestrian friendliness. It ranked 7th worst in a 2016 Smart Growth America study of major metropolitan areas for cyclist safety,[lxxv] and although the City of Tampa added approximately 90 miles of bike lanes during Mayor Bob Buckhorn's tenure, the failure of this high-profile project stung. Christina Acosta, executive director of the nonprofit advocacy group Walk Bike Tampa, called the city's decision a "huge disappointment."

"We are befuddled as to why the city didn't opt to make Bay to Bay better and safer," Acosta said. "This was supposed to be about creating a neighborhood environment where small businesses can thrive."[lxxvi]

I don't think the situation is befuddling at all. Most people, including otherwise forward-thinking public figures, still see cycling as a recreational activity and not as a legitimate mode of transportation. Would you ever consider telling drivers that they should just use another street to get to where they wanted to go? We know how to design better transportation infrastructure, but we have got to find new ways to sell it to our communities for it to really make a difference.

Part of the problem is a public policy and governance approach. In the Palo Alto area in 2016, Keene told me, regional city managers formed the Managers Mobility Partnership, consisting of Redwood City, Menlo Park, Palo Alto, Mountain View, and Stanford University.[lxxvii] The idea was to coordinate their efforts to ensure that cyclists had a seamless and consistent experience as they commuted from city to city via their bikes. Together, they pledged to seek out opportunities for coordination and to look for potential gaps in services that might discourage folks from using the existing infrastructure for biking.

Other changes must target the culture of transit. One approach is to encourage those who have not been on a bike in a long time to get on and ride through a part of their city. Efforts such as these need to be hosted and managed by the bike advocacy community. You can't just expect people who have not ridden a bike in years to be comfortable on a bike or even have access to a bike.

A few years ago, I spoke at a regional planning conference in downtown Columbus, Ohio. The day prior to my opening keynote, the conference had hosted a bike tour of downtown, which I joined. I watched as many of the participants gingerly mounted their bikes and set off on unsteady wheels. Within a few minutes, everyone was laughing and doing just fine. Riding a bike really is just like riding a bike, but that doesn't mean people are going to be instantly comfortable with the idea. Help them out, provide the bikes and the group leaders to show them how to ride in their city safely. This will give residents that much-needed perspective on the experience of riding in their city. It will likely prove to be illuminating, as they realize cycling is fun and easy to do. They will also realize that being out there on a bike can be scary, too, and maybe the next time they pass a cyclist or cross a bike lane, they will be a bit more aware and considerate of people on bikes.

Special events such as the Cyclovia concept from Latin America can significantly change the culture. "Cyclovia" means "bikeway" in Spanish, and the event has its origins in Colombia in the 1970s. It began when the City of Bogotá closed a roadway on a weekend and made it into a bicycle pathway for a few hours. People were invited to come down with their families and go for a leisurely and safe bike ride. The concept proved wildly popular and the Cyclovia became a weekly event. Today, every Sunday in Bogotá, Cali, Medellín, and many other Columbian cities, thousands of people come out and ride their bikes. Cities all over the world have copied the idea, and hundreds of similar events have happened across the entire United States.

These events bring out families and introduce, or re-introduce, them to the simple pleasure of riding a bike. This has the nice side benefit of potentially improving community health and wellness. Overall, it raises the profile of cycling in the community, creates more support for cycling infrastructure, and helps decenter the car in transit culture.

Slow Roll Detroit started out as a weekly bike ride

among friends. In 2010, co-founders Jason Hall and Mike MacKool invited a few friends to meet for a bike ride through some of Detroit's most interesting neighborhoods. Their weekly Monday-night ride developed into an unofficial tour of what was cool and interesting in the city, hosted by Hall and MacKool. The popularity of the rides quickly grew. By 2015, the weekly rides attracted a couple thousand riders and effectively shut down streets as they passed through. This growth necessitated Slow Roll becoming a membership-based organization that included permits and police escorts for the ride. The rides themselves became spectacles as people dressed in costumes, decorated their bikes, and generally made the event into a party on two wheels. Jason Hall became a bit of a celebrity as he and Slow Roll were featured on an Apple commercial, and other cities adopted the Slow Roll model.

What is interesting to me about Slow Roll is that it really is a community development project, not a cycling project. It uses cycling as a method to connect people and introduce them to parts of their city, which is brilliant. While it is not specifically designed to address car culture, the project has been able to bring out thousands of riders on a regular basis to ride their city and, for better or worse, to bring cycling to the attention of drivers and city leadership. Slow Roll is about changing the emotional state of the city.

Culture Shift – Be the Change

In the culture of road sharing and transportation, cars and drivers are the main actors. There are just more of them, and their power—both literal and figurative—is hugely disproportionate to the other players'. Those of us who are drivers, thus bear the lion's share of responsibility for the change that must happen. However, we cannot let the cycling community off the hook, as there is much we need to do to change the culture on the road. The first and foremost of these changes is for everyone involved to start obeying traffic laws.

I have a confession to make. I used to be one of those Lycra-clad cyclists racing down the roads with a peloton of other cyclists. We certainly felt safer by riding in a pack, but we also routinely broke traffic laws. We would ride through stop signs, and even red lights, because if the first rider made it through, the rest of us had to follow them. We almost never signaled our turns. I know we annoyed drivers. Today I see cyclists doing similar things as they blow through red lights, jump curbs and even go the wrong way down one-way streets. I know they think they are aware of traffic and their surroundings, and that they are just taking advantage of the environment. Perhaps true, but what they are really doing is confirming drivers' worst attitudes toward cyclists. "These idiots are weaving in and out of traffic" or "they just ran the light," drivers may think, justifiably. I know most cyclists obey the laws (or at least most of the laws), but because those who do break the rules are often much more visible, the problem feels widespread. Every time we break the rules on our bikes, we foment the notion in the heads of drivers that bikes don't belong. Perhaps on a subconscious level, we act out that expectation as cyclists. We would never (hopefully) get in our car and flout the rules of the road the way we do when we get on a bike.

Copenhagen, the capital city of Denmark, is often pointed to by bike advocates and transportation experts as the benchmark for cycling and bicycle infrastructure. The city has been voted the most bike-friendly city in the world, and 43% of its citizens commute via bicycle.[lxxviii] The city also has an incredibly structured and disciplined cycling community. To take to the road on a bike, you act like you would in a car. You stop, you signal, you pass on the left, and every bike is required to have lights and reflectors. I know that this much regulation is likely to rankle many Americans, and perhaps we are not there yet, but the notion of acting like we belong on the road is critical. Jim Keene told me that he often yells at other cyclists when they break the rules. "You are making it harder for all of us," he says.

Enter Scooters

As I write this, the current hot trend in urban transportation is not the driverless car or the dock-less bike share, but rather the old school scooter. Electric scooters for rent are popping up in cities all over North America and many other parts of the world. Their appeal stems from being small, inexpensive, easy to park, and simple enough that most able-bodied people can operate one. Rental rates are roughly $1 plus $0.15 per mile, and the entire transaction is handled through an app on your smartphone. Maximum speeds are about 15 mph, and a single battery charge can take a scooter upwards of thirty miles. And these scooters are dock-less, requiring nothing more than a kickstand, instead of the centralized station characteristic of the first generation of bike share programs.

Two California start-ups are leading the way. Bird and Lime are the Uber and Lyft of the electric scooter world. Bird launched in September 2017 in eighteen U.S. cities, and Lime came online in May 2018 in 65 U.S. cities—as well as Paris, Berlin and Zurich. Lime received a funding infusion of $335 million in July 2018 that included tech giants Uber and Google's parent company Alphabet.[lxxix] Bird has raised more than $300 million, and both start-ups are each valued at over a billion dollars. Notably, Uber also acquired bike share company JUMP in 2018 for an estimated $200 million.[lxxx] The future appears to have two wheels.

Many are saying that scooters will revolutionize urban transit, which is certainly a possibility. In 2001, when the Segway launched, similar expressions about it were made by some very smart people. Steve Jobs said that cities would be designed around it.[lxxxi] Clearly, that did not happen; other than the occasional flock of tourists or airport security guards on Segways, you don't see the vehicle much these days. Regardless of whether scooters will be the next big thing, cities have rapidly responded to their introduction—likely because they were caught so flat-footed by the appearance of Uber and Lyft a few years ago. In contrast, the scooter companies have not been very communicative or cooperative with the initial cities they located in. Mostly, they just dumped hundreds of scooters on city sidewalks and said have at it. Understandably, many cities were not pleased and took legal action against them. In 2017, Bird settled a lawsuit in its hometown of Santa Monica, California, for operating without the proper licenses. San Francisco temporarily banned scooters, as have Denver[lxxxii] and Nashville,[lxxxiii] pending the creation of a regulatory framework for their operation on busy city sidewalks. It is this framework that will be the key issue. Jeff Bezos, CEO of Amazon, once said of the Segway that the key question was, "Are people going to be allowed to use it?"[lxxxiv]

City councils all over the country will be challenged by this latest addition to the mobility menu. Some will look to regulate scooters like a bicycle. Others will see young hipsters riding them and think they are more like the reviled skateboard and may seek to ban them altogether. Taxi companies, already taking a hit from ride share platforms, will see scooters as a further threat. Other technology ventures, such as Zip Car and Car2Go, will see them as a threat as well. There are already lawsuits alleging injuries and negligence by the scooter companies.[lxxxv] The companies themselves are challenging existing rules and regulations. In California, motorized vehicles (including electric scooters) are not permitted to operate on sidewalks and require a helmet when riding. Bird has introduced a bill into the California legislature that looks to repeal those provisions for scooters.[lxxxvi]

Bird has also provided some thought-provoking information that may also cause cities to pause in their zeal to regulate or eliminate scooters. As I write in early 2019, Bird claims that in Santa Monica alone, the availability of its scooters has "prevented" 1.6 million miles of driving.[lxxxvii] They can track the usage of their scooters, so I believe the total miles they claim—but whether using a scooter stopped someone from getting into a car is another matter. Nonetheless, that number is impressive, and I am certain that the use of scooters has led to less car miles. If even a half or a third of 1.6 million miles is true, that portends some very real opportunities for cities.

Efforts to regulate scooters, while well-meaning, are missing the underlying emotional issue—fear of the car. Scooter companies want to use sidewalks because they know that riders are going to be afraid (justifiably so) of being in traffic with cars. This means we are putting even more congestion on our sidewalks and undermining the very thing we are trying to promote—alternative, non-automotive transportation options. If we push all those options into one realm (the sidewalk), we are forcing them to compete for a severely limited space and *not* addressing the fundamental behavior that we should be seeking to change, i.e., encouraging people to drive less.

Why are we so afraid to ask drivers to modify their behavior? I believe our reluctance resides in the belief that almost everybody drives or, more likely, the belief that everybody who drives spends more, votes more, simply matters more than those who do not have a car. I see a huge underlying class bias here. Public transportation is not as well-funded as it should be because of the perception that poor people use public transportation. Bicycle infrastructure is cute, but only hipsters and people who can't afford cars will use it.

Because those who use alternative transportation seem to matter less, we are far more comfortable modifying their behaviors than we are at challenging the primacy of the car. This has got to change.

When cars dominate the city and we literally fear them, it feels like the city is for the car. I believe that our car-centered design has had the unintended consequence of diminishing us and our connection to our places. We become strangers in Car Town. If you don't feel welcome and accommodated, it makes an emotional connection that much more difficult.

As long as we see transportation infrastructure as merely engineering to get (mostly) cars from point A to point B as efficiently as possible, we will miss out on massive opportunities to remake our places to serve a higher purpose. A walkable, bikeable, or scoot-able city suggests a more physically, socially, and emotionally balanced place where people have designated areas of primacy (downtowns, residential streets), and cars have their place, too (highways, boulevards). This feels fair—that we as citizens have access to the benefits and resources of our city. As human beings, we have a deep appreciation of the concept of fairness. Social scientists call it "distributive justice," our propensity to look for a socially just manner of distributing goods and services in our society. This is not an argument for wealth redistribution or socialism, or any other hot button political issue that the words "socially just" may stir up. It is a simple declaration that when people feel more included and part of their city, even in the most modest of ways, we improve the nature of the relationship between city and citizen.

A Word About Autonomous Vehicles

Commuting, parking and potholes—three emotional hot buttons that are directly linked to our car culture. As noted above, car culture is changing with emerging generational attitudes, but the arrival of autonomous vehicles will have a huge impact on our emotional relationships with our places. Everywhere I go, everyone who works in every discipline related to urban planning, placemaking, economic development, technology and talent attraction—is talking about these vehicles. They will rewrite our development playbooks, our municipal codes, our planning guidelines, our insurance laws, and our very definitions of transportation. Think about it—is something still a car if you don't drive it? Is it more of a train but without the track? Will our children ever buy a vehicle? Will they ever need to get a driver's license? These are questions that will need to be addressed. The real question is, "When?"

My first experience with autonomous vehicles occurred in early 2018 when I visited Phoenix, Arizona. As my friend Lorenzo Perez showed me around his city, he pointed out several autonomous vehicles on the road. He told me that they were everywhere in Phoenix. This was a conscious effort by the leadership in Arizona to court technology companies from California. The state provided incentives, including changes to law, that allowed for large-scale testing of autonomous vehicles in Arizona. The result was a huge influx of companies, along with their engineers and designers, as they deployed vehicles for real world testing. I was fascinated to watch these vehicles in traffic. The main difference I noticed was that they actually signaled to change lanes—no human driver does that!

What will cities look like when, instead of owning a car, we simply summon an autonomous ride-share to chauffer us to work? Some business leaders, including Tesla founder Elon Musk, have suggested that our use of cars and car-based services will increase because it will be more pleasant and productive to interact with cars. This increased interest could lead to more traffic congestion. Even if that turns out to be true (and the length of our commute doesn't change or even grows worse), our emotional experience of the commute could be radically different. Instead of being behind the wheel and under the continual stress of driving, we will sit in the backseat with our phones and laptops, perhaps working, perhaps watching the latest binge-worthy Netflix show. Many believe we won't sit in nearly as much gridlock, as autonomous vehicles are expected to merge and flow much more seamlessly than human-driven vehicles. A commute could become "me-time." Once we arrive at our destination, we won't worry about parking; we'll simply exit the vehicle, and off it goes to its next fare. And the pothole? If we hit one, we won't care nearly as much. Perhaps the autonomous vehicle even registered its exact location and has already reported it to the appropriate government department for repair.

I look forward to this becoming a reality but know that, even in this utopian scenario, we must anticipate a full spectrum of users, including those less tech savvy and even fearful of a driverless experience. Technology is both the great leveler and the great divider in our communities. It falls upon us, as emotionally savvy place makers, to understand and account for such disparity. Our solutions, especially to something as foundational as transportation, must be fair, equitable, and accessible to diverse communities, lest we create another transportation system that produces an entirely new set of societal, economic, and emotional problems- or reproduces the same old ones.

CHAPTER 3 – PARKS, GREEN SPACE & THE EMOTIONAL HEALTH OF A CITY

I opened this book with the idea of a new question to be asked about how a place feels to us. That question opens the door to conversations and approaches to placemaking that we have overlooked. It recognizes that our sense of place is rooted in this emotional infrastructure. One of the most important parts of that emotional infrastructure—and amongst the least funded and under-appreciated aspects of our places (at least by our leaders)—is also the most beloved, healthy, and egalitarian aspects of our community. I am speaking about our parks and greenways.

It has become canon in our cities that parks are good for their communities. They improve the physical, mental and emotional health of the people in the community. I describe parks and green spaces as the healthy lungs of vibrant city. They increase property values and they are good for the environment and climate. Parks are good. They are also expensive and do require large amounts of highly specialized knowledge to maintain. Because they are also more passive than, say, a commercial district, there is the notion that they can keep doing what they do, without support or resources. After all, the trees will continue to grow whether we have park rangers or arborists on staff. When budgets are allocated, parks are easily cut because they are not seen as essential to the function and success of cities. It is easy to calculate how much tax revenue a Wal-Mart Super Center brings in; it is harder to put a monetary value on the neighborhood park. Consequently, parks are seen as a debit on the economic ledger of our cities and not an asset. This underscores the limitation of single bottom line thinking in our cities.

What counts and how we count it

The very measures by which we judge the success or failure of parks and green space is woefully insufficient. One frequently deployed metric is usage: how many people come in and out of the park, use the pool, or workout in the community center. Usage should be a starting point and only one aspect of what we look at in understanding the role of parks. Measuring a park's value by usage is like saying the number of times you kiss your partner is the measure of your love for them. There may be some correlation, but to reduce love to a number insults the very idea of love and, worst of all, makes it seem like love is something that should be measured, metered, and manufactured.

Amanda Burden, a former New York City Planning Director for former Mayor Michael Bloomberg, said of parks and public spaces that they "have power. It's not just the number of people using them, it's the even greater number of people who feel better about their city just knowing that they are there. Public space can change how you live in a city, how you feel about a city, whether you choose one city over another, and public space is one of the most important reasons why you stay in a city."[i] A park may not prevent my car from getting broken into, but the park helps me feel better, and reminds me of the good and the lovable elements of my city. But what if a park could prevent crime? A growing body of evidence suggests this very effect.

A 2015 study led by the USDA Forest Service looked at greenspace in Youngstown, Ohio over a five-year period and noted that well maintained greenspaces, ones that were mowed and kept clean, compared to less maintained greenspaces in the city had noticeably lower property crimes in them[lxxxviii]. And green spaces and parks that were actually maintained and cared for the neighboring communities had lower incidents of violent crime.[lxxxix] This should not be surprising as it is a natural extension of Jane Jacob's concept of the "eyes of strangers on the street" being an antidote to crime and bad behavior. A well-maintained space is more likely to be used or simply looked at, while a poorly maintained and neglected space is an eyesore and one you will likely avoid if you can. A 2015 report from the journal *Landscape and Urban Planning* noted that in a Baltimore study of yards and greenspace, the "factors most strongly tied to more crime were the number of small street trees, litter, uncut lawn, and a dried-out lawn."[xc]

There was also a positive correlation that supports the idea that visible maintenance of shared spaces presents "a sign of social capital and cohesion that might deter criminals."[xci]

Cities spend enormous amounts of money on police and safety every year. Yet, if we start to look at how we invest our money in our places through this emotional infrastructure lens, we might see that some less obvious, almost oblique investments in things, such as our parks and green spaces, might help to reduce those critical challenges. We might be better able to justify the costs of parks and turn them from a nice to have to a must-have investment for our places.

In my previous book, *Love Where You Live,* I argued that while everything has a cost, everything also has a value-- and that the two are most often not the same. Costs are generally easy to quantify, while assessing the value of something often requires a different lens or methodology. The cost of a public park is evident; the value of that park to its community is much harder to encapsulate. Intuitively, we understand the value of these spaces, but because parks and green spaces appear passive, they don't capture our attention as much. Some have therefore made the point that massive, iconic parks such as Millennium Park in Chicago are necessary to help make the case for the value of these spaces.

Begun in 1997 and initially budgeted at $150 million, the effort to build Millennium Park ran four years behind schedule and ended up costing $475 million, with taxpayers in Chicago paying over $270 million, and the rest coming from private and corporate donors. On paper, $270 million is a hard number for leaders to wrap their heads and their political lives around. Yet, today, that investment seems visionary. The park is a multiple award-winning public place, including "Best Public Space" by Travel & Leisure magazine,[xcii] and a case study in the value of iconic parks and public art. This very success has made some city leaders blind to, or at the very least disinterested in, small-scale investments in public spaces, parks, and public art. Like the grand opening of a new building, an iconic park or public space attracts a lot of attention. It is a very visible success story that leaders can point to and say "I did that" during the next election campaign. It is much harder to point to a refurbished playground or the well-maintained grass at a neighborhood park and declare victory. Yet politicians should do precisely this!

The success of large-scale projects, like Millennium Park, or the High Line in New York City, have shown that these projects can generate tremendous excitement for cities. Politicians and citizens alike can point to such projects and say, "Yes, we want one." Ironically, it becomes easier to fund large scale projects because of this attention. Big projects transect multiple areas of interest—municipal, corporate, and philanthropic—and these entities line up to become part of the process. Over 40% of Millennium Park was funded by private donors—over $200 million.[ii]

Yet repainting the neighborhood playground is a challenge. Focusing on the iconic has detracted from the need and importance of small, neighborhood parks for communities. But some research tells a different story. The City of Chicago parks department participated in a study[iii] that looked at the relative economic impacts of the city's parks, ranging from Millennium Park down to the smallest parks in their system. What they found was surprising. Parks Department CEO Michael Kelly told me that the small parks had a proportionately larger impact on their local neighborhood economies than the mega Millennium Park. Of course, he said that Millennium Park's impact stretched into the tourism and convention realm as well, but for localized impact on the residents of neighborhoods, the small parks punched well above their weight. The study, called *The Power of Parks*, noted that overall property values of residences within .15 miles (roughly a block and half) of a park had an increase of 1.5%—value directly attributable to parks. But the relative and overall absolute increase of value from the pocket parks was more than 50% greater than the so-called "magnet parks" such as Millennium Park.[xciii]

Perhaps some of the fault for our fixation on large-scale parks lies with one of the legends of city building. Daniel Burnham (1846-1912), the American architect and urban planner, is famous for his work on the 1893 Chicago World's Fair and his 1909 Plan for Chicago. He worked at truly heroic scale and is credited with the well-known quote, "Make no little plans. They have no magic to stir men's blood and probably will not themselves be realized." That is a memorable sentiment, but one that has perhaps been too deeply indoctrinated among our planners, designers and architects, and thus by extension, among the policy makers who govern their work. Big plans, big parks, big projects, when completed, even when merely announced, carry a perceived weight and significance that may inadvertently suck the air out of the room for smaller, localized projects.

A small "pocket" park may be a blip on the municipal radar but a defining aspect of a particular neighborhood's identity. It can be the place where people meet, where their kids play, where they walk their dogs, or simply people-watch. Such small-scale parks are the psychic centers of neighborhoods, and if they are healthy, well-maintained, and loved, that attitude carries over to the neighborhood as a whole. Small investments of money, time, and attention can pay big dividends for all. Failure to care for such spaces carries the corresponding negative implications for their communities. Even a coat of paint or a bit of landscaping can bring significant uptick in usage and the perceived value of a park.

For each big project, we need dozens, perhaps even hundreds, of smaller projects to fill in the spaces between. A city with one great, iconic park is not much of a city to the

95% of the population who may not live in close proximity to that park. This is the thinking by the Trust for Public Land (TPL) in conjunction with the National Recreation & Parks Association and the Urban Land Institute, which has initiated a nationwide challenge to cities called the "10-Minute Walk." The core idea is that every American deserves a park within a 10 minute walk (about half a mile) from where they live. Their research showed that one-third of Americans don't have that level of access to a park. They have begun the process of securing commitments from mayors and city managers to include the goal in their future planning efforts. By the fall of 2018, over 200 cities had committed to this goal[iv]. It also provides cities a clear and measurable metric for success in their efforts beyond more blunt measures such as total acreage or spending. This measure feels fairer and more equitable as it encourages decentralization of the investments and "spreads the love" around.

My hometown of St. Petersburg, Florida, does quite well in the rankings, with 74% of its residents living within the 10-minute walk range. New York City has 97% of its residents covered, while other dynamic cities such as Columbus, Ohio, come in at 52% coverage. The measure is not perfect. Dense, less car-centric cities such as New York and San Francisco will fare better in this calculus than Columbus, which has been built around the car. The measure also doesn't account for the relative quality of the park, but it does provide a necessary starting point for future planning decisions. More importantly, it assumes an equity mindset that is much needed in our civic thinking.

Parks Without Borders

One of the leaders in the conversation about equity and public space has been New York City and its parks commissioner, Mitchell Silver. I first met Silver in 2015 in Grand Rapids, Michigan. We were invited to share a stage and talk about placemaking from our different perspectives. I found in Silver a harmonious voice on the topic I was speaking about—the intangible, soft, human element of place-making that is often overlooked in our mechanistic, engineered approach to development. The event was so well received that we were invited to do another joint presentation in Florida later that year. Silver was appointed as New York City Parks Commissioner in 2014 by Mayor Bill de Blasio. Unlike most parks officials, Silver comes from a planning background, having served as planning director for Raleigh, North Carolina, and as a former president of the American Planning

Association. His approach and orientation to the unique role parks and green spaces play in a city has been evident in the work that his department has spearheaded over the past several years.

In 2015, Silver's staff initiated a program called "Parks Without Borders," which re-imagined the entryways and perimeters of eight key parks as a test case. What they did was simple yet revolutionary. They took down fences. Said Silver during our conversation, "as an urban planner, it's important to me to create seamless public realms... We are lowering or removing perimeter fences in parks throughout the city. This makes our parks more open and welcoming. Parks should flow into the surrounding sidewalks, not be cordoned off with tall, intimidating fences."[v]

Fences exist for many reasons, safety being one of the most obvious. We cordon off spaces and define their usages with a bright line of demarcation—a fence. Fences also serve as borders of authority and ownership, both legal and perceived. When a fence goes around a park, it says, in no uncertain terms—this is the park's space and, therefore, the Parks Department's space. Municipal departments, like competing departments in a corporation or reality TV show rivals, are competitive and highly protective of what they see as their dominion. Functionally, this is an efficient way to separate the vast amount of work that must be done in every city. It also puts brackets and blinders on our people as they believe their authority and responsibility ends with the fence. By taking down the fences, Silver is thinking beyond the limits of his office and his official mandate, and that is a wonderful thing. Silver often calls himself the "Commissioner of Fun"[lvi] which inherently breaks down the walls and invites new thinking to the process. Recognizing a responsibility (fun, beauty, inclusion) and an opportunity beyond your silo helps us get beyond balkanized solutions that address one aspect of a city, often to the detriment to another part. When we are creating more holistic and multi-disciplinary approaches and solutions, we are often tangentially addressing our most vexing and complicated problems.

Another example of working beyond the confines of the department comes from the summer of 2018, when Silver and his team launched the "Cool Pools" initiative, an effort to refurbish and refresh many of the city's public pools. "We set out to make public pools look fresh and inviting by adding bright paint colors, fun wall art, cabanas, lounge chairs, umbrellas, and plants. As a result, we increased attendance by 20% so far this season, and the feedback has been extremely positive," Silver said.[vii] One can look at this as a nice success story, but there is an underlying issue that permeates the work we do in our cities that needs to brought to the forefront: social equity. Think about who uses public pools in the city—families and kids who may not be able to afford a private gym, a country club or a beach vacation. Investing in these public amenities is investing in the lives of those who live at the margins of our communities.

The Equity Elephant in the Room

We have discussed the implications of the growing income and opportunity gap in our country in prior chapters. This manifests in many ways, including the militant anti-gentrification movement, transit decisions that starve public options, and housing policies that require affordable housing for development. Into this increasingly dire environment, one area of positivity is our public parks and green spaces. Public parks, as free and universally accessible amenities in cities, are some of the most equitable and egalitarian elements in places. Commissioner Silver has said, "One of my top priorities is making our parks system equitable. That means making sure that every neighborhood—especially historically underserved neighborhoods—have a quality park that is safe and well-maintained."[viii] When people have access to a park, not even a great park, but just a good, functional and clean park, they will feel better about their city. Give them a great park, with fun amenities and beautiful environs, and people will feel included and loved by their city.

There are some who hear the term "social equity" and believe it is a mask for wealth redistribution or even socialism. To me social equity is about a baseline of acceptable standards in our communities and recognizing that we all should have access to certain fundamental things. The "10-Minute Walk" initiative is such a minimum standard. Clean air and water also come to mind, and everyone seems to be on board with these. Though as evinced by the tragedy in Flint, Michigan's water system, we still can fall short of that goal. Other concepts, such as access to housing or Universal Basic Income, are more controversial because they have a significant economic component and when economics are involved, there are lots of competing interests. But there should be some other fundamentals in this mix as well. How about access to beauty? Does being poor mean that you have to settle for utilitarian, battleship grey options? How about access to green spaces and natural environments? Do trees and flower boxes only exist in the middle and upper class neighborhoods? Hopefully we can all agree that this should not be the case.

Some will argue that these are *nice to have*, but not *necessary to have* in the grand scheme of things; that jobs and infrastructure like roads and sewers are the standard to which we build. My contention is that these are symbiotic and must be seen as interconnected. They need not be labeled as equals, but both must be seen as requirements and prerequisites for growth and development. A human being must have water to survive. A few days without and you will die. A human being must also have Vitamin C, a micro trace element in our food, or a few weeks out you will have scurvy, a progressively degenerative disease. Continued lack of this micro element will result in death. A job is like the water, but beauty and green spaces are the Vitamin C that keep us healthy and strong.

There is also growing scientific evidence that green space and access to nature is more important than we ever thought. Biophilia is a term first used by German social scientist Erich Fromm in 1964[ix]. The term means "love of life or living systems." It is a concept that E. O. Wilson, known as the "father of biodiversity"[x], expanded upon in his book, *The Biophilia Hypothesis*.

Wilson suggested that as human beings we have the urge to associate and interact with other life forms.[xi] Philias, being the opposite of phobias (fears) indicate a natural human attraction to nature and its myriad forms. Consider the importance of that idea – that we as human beings are hardwired to desire, and thus seek out, nature and natural settings. We don't just like the view of the forest, the lake or the valley, we actually need it. Greening our cities goes from being a nice or good idea to becoming an essential one. Moreover, it suggests that the way we have approached integrating nature and green space into our cities is not designed for how we truly want to interact with them.

In his excellent book, *The Happy City*, author Charles Montgomery explores the myriad effects our built environments have upon our physical and mental health. He offers several approaches for rethinking and remaking our cities, but one that struck me in particular was his discussion on biological complexity. Montgomery suggests that allowing for more biodiversity or "messiness" in our urban design would promote this biophilic response in citizens, making them happier and more connected to their environment. Happier and more emotionally engaged citizens seems like an obvious good, so why would cities not consider this approach more fully? Because it flies in the face of the underlying belief system about our green space in cities.

Our sense of green space is orderly lawns and gardens, carefully trimmed trees and urban flower beds. Don't get me wrong, these are wonderful and I believe necessary parts of any city. But this emerging biophilic science now suggests that we respond better to more organic environments. Apparently, our brains seek diverse, more interesting, more complex environments and ecosystems. We want things that "pack a bigger punch than... a manicured patch of grass, because they are more likely to draw us into the levels of involuntary attention that are so soothing."[xii] Montgomery notes that "sterile lawns and token trees" are "hollow calories for our nature-craving brain."[xiii]

Urban planners have long recognized the need for green space in our cities. Even before Daniel Burnham and the City Beautiful Movement, planners were including parks and green space in their designs. However, they would seek to "tame" that wildness and make the space into a neat, clean, and safe option. They would also design it to maximize the value of the nearby built environment. An aesthetically pleasing park across from your residential development made for a much more valuable property. Moreover, our sense of urban planning neatly puts elements into appropriate containers. Residential here, commercial here, industrial goes way over there. It uses green space to create neat buffer zones or islands in the overall scheme of the city. Then we put fences around those same parks to control the usages! Green space was viewed as a necessary element but hardly the curative for our urban existence that it now seems to be.

Parks and green space make us healthier, happier, more connected to our community and each other. They also increase economic value[xciv], reduce crime[xcv], increase social equity[xcvi], and fundamentally make us feel we are part of a place. That is foundational emotional infrastructure. They are the closest thing to a magic bullet in a city's arsenal. There are few things more universally loved in a city than its parks, and I believe we are vastly under-utilizing them in our strategies and tactics for making better places. We need to break down the historic and institutional barriers and unleash the green goodness of our parks upon our cities.

A new administrative approach

In early 2016, I visited South Bend, Indiana, at the invitation of Aaron Perri, then executive director of the city's downtown association. Perri was in the process of leaving the downtown association for a new position created specifically for him by South Bend Mayor Pete Buttigieg (pronounced "boot-edge-edge"). "Mayor Pete," as many know him, was elected in 2011. Then 29-years old, Buttigieg became the youngest mayor of an American city with a population of 100,000 or more. Since then, he has been lauded by many organizations for his visionary thinking and approach to government. One of his signature endeavors - code-named "Project Q - has been to initiate significant infrastructural improvements to South Bend.

Tapped by Buttigieg to lead Project Q, Perri was going to merge three city departments: parks and recreation, arts and culture, and venues, the latter inclusive of the city's performing arts center and convention center. The underlying theory was that these departments were central to quality of life in South Bend—hence the "q" in Project Q. Perri was selected for his diverse experience, which prior to running the downtown association had included a stint as a venues manager and the creator-producer of a series of successful community events. Perri was a classic citizen "co-creator" who had moved from the grassroots into city government. The mayor realized that selecting someone from within the three existing departments could prevent outside-the-box thinking, so he needed a talented outsider who was not beholden to any particular discipline or approach. He found that person in Perri.

Reconstituted as the Department of Venues, Parks & Arts, Perri and his team have begun a $51 million renovation in the city's park infrastructure. Years of deferred maintenance had taken a toll on all the department's assets, but particularly on the iconic downtown Howard Park. This 12-acre park sits in the center of South Bend along its riverfront and is central to the identity of the city. But in addition to the big park, the city was investing in smaller parks in marginalized neighborhoods of the city. West of the river, the first renovations occurred in LaSalle Park and included installing the only bike repair shop on the west side of the city, so that neighborhood kids could learn to repair bicycles. The city partnered with Charles Jenkins, known locally as "the bike man" because he has been repairing bikes in the neighborhood for years[xcvii]. Perri hopes that these types of interventions will promote the acquisition of life skills for youth and maybe even business opportunities for the community.[xiv] This approach, he told me, is about "increasing social equity."

Some larger cities and counties have well-established departments encompassing these and other functions into one organizational body. Now, we see smaller cities intentionally moving towards this integrated approach to quality of life issues and beginning to initiate their own versions of Project Q, including Mesa, Ariz., Spokane, Wash., and Lansing, Mich. Perri tells me he gets calls every week from other cities asking about the work they are doing in South Bend. I hope this interest portends a revision of thinking in city government, and the advent of more interdisciplinary teams and departments capable of wrestling with big, hairy problems that refuse to fall neatly into a single department. These days, I often observe cities pulling their leadership together to surround and address such complex problems. Thus far, most have stopped short of re-organizing fundamental structures to hardwire these new approaches, but I can see it coming. As cities like South Bend lead the way and find the pitfalls and the hidden opportunities, we will begin to rewrite the very organizational charts that have defined our civic structures for over a century.

Peter Kageyama

CHAPTER 4 – CHANGING DOWNTOWN RETAIL

As a kid growing up in Akron, Ohio, I recall going shopping downtown with my grandmother. She never learned to drive a car, so we took the bus down Market Street to the heart of downtown Akron, aptly named Main Street. There were two grand old department stores on Main Street, Polsky's and O'Neil's, where we would shop (usually for school clothes—not my favorite, but it was still an adventure) and get lunch at one of their food counters. By the 1970's, even my childhood eyes could tell that these stores were a shadow of their former selves, though their old-fashioned escalators still felt majestic to a kid. Downtown retail had followed the urban outmigration to the suburbs, where gleaming new shopping malls were cropping up. So passed a generation of downtown retail. Soon the suburban mall offered so many options and conveniences that the thought of going downtown for any purpose felt positively antiquated.

Retail is the largest private sector employer in the United States, directly and indirectly accounting for 42 million jobs.[xcviii] In Europe, retail accounts for 15% of employment, or some 33 million jobs.[xcix] It's not too much of a stretch to say that retail policy is as impactful to the lives of our cities as public policy.

Consider the flight of city residents to the suburbs in the later part of the 20th century. That movement of people was largely driven by commercial zoning, land and tax policies designed to incentivize malls and big box retail stores in the increasingly suburban areas. Of course, there is a chicken-and-egg reality here, with each change begetting and fueling the other, but hindsight has made clear the interdependence of retail policies, transportation policies and economic development in shaping how we live. Changes to the retail landscape supported and amplified other policies related to civic life and helped beget the suburbs as we know them.

Why should we care where people spend their money? Money spent at the mall, the outlet store, the big box retail chain or downtown is still counted the same way in our city's economic development scorecard, isn't it? Yes—and that is the fundamental limitation of one of our key measures of the success of cities. On the metaphorical ledger that is our economic development scorecard, a dollar is a dollar, and in the financial calculus of our cities, where it is spent matters very little so long as it is spent within your geographic boundaries. Urban planners, business leaders, and elected officials read the social and cultural portents, saw the demographic shift away from urban areas towards the developing suburbs, and then accelerated that shift with their policy decisions. Communities and those gatekeepers of our economic development were more than happy to locate the businesses anywhere they wanted and anywhere they thought they would fit, with little or no thought towards the externalities those financial decisions created.

However, where money is spent matters in the emotional calculus of our communities, because each transaction has impacts beyond the literal sale. Study after study shows[c] that when people spend money at locally owned businesses, more of that money stays within a community. That local money in turn feeds networks that create jobs, start-up businesses and even helps reduce economic inequality.[ci]

Ed McMahon, a Senior Fellow with the Urban Land Institute, put it succinctly, "Downtowns are the heart and soul of a community. If you don't have a healthy downtown you simply don't have a healthy city or town."[cii] I have called downtowns the "psychic centers" of places. Even if you live in the suburbs of your city and don't interact regularly with your downtown, it still is the image you think of when you think of your city and it has a huge impact on the overall economic vitality of your entire region. A successful downtown results in a sense of vibrancy that is essential to the infrastructure of feeling in our places.

Today we are more interested in downtowns than ever, and retail is returning to these urban centers. Not in its previous form—the grand department store of my childhood is most likely gone for good—but in new, emergent, and sometimes surprising ways that are challenging the ability of cities to adapt and re-imagine the fundamental nature of retail. To accommodate the flow of occupancy and investment back into city centers, we need to consider creating a regulatory environment, including zoning and tax policies, that fosters emerging urban retail. Knowing what we know now, we would be remiss if we did not note this unique opportunity to ask deeper questions and include something beyond pure economics in our thinking. How can we use retail behavior and consumerism to better shape our cities and make them into something more than epicenters of trade?

Several years ago, I had the occasion to meet Roger

Brooks at an event in Greenville, South Carolina. Brooks is widely recognized as *the* downtown retail guru, and with his firm, Destination Development Association, has worked with downtowns all over North America. Brooks has developed a simple formula for successful downtowns. He calls it 10/10/10: "Ten places that serve food. Ten places that are destination retail shops, whether they're galleries or wine stores. And then of those twenty, at least ten are open after 6 p.m." Downtowns, he continued, "are not where we go to buy socks, hosiery, underwear, those things. Downtowns are about where we go after work and on weekends." What he has outlined here is something beyond pure economics, and instead paints a picture of a highly programmed and designed experience.

Developing a downtown program

So, if it's as simple as 10/10/10, what keeps cities from having successful downtowns? Part of the problem is the way we have thought of "downtown," historically. In the past, downtown was a center for commerce and business. We love that there are law offices, insurance companies, banks and other premium rent-paying entities in our downtowns. But these enterprises are not actually creating the vibrancy that downtowns need to succeed. When we look at who else is in downtown, we may also be talking about some traditional retailers who have hung on over the years. These retailers have become habituated to the idea that they close at 5 p.m. or 6 p.m., when the business community leaves. But as Brooks practically shouted with excitement during our conversation, "the big deal, the big deal, is that 70% of all consumer retail spending takes place after 6 p.m."

Smart cities, often through their downtown development agencies or Main Street programs, have recognized that cultural programming plays a critical role in getting and keeping more people downtown consistently. Brooks recommends a goal of 250 days out of the year. Many cities have recognized this need and have already put in place the personnel and infrastructure to achieve a critical mass of programming. Yet there are still some elements within the structure and thinking of our cities that work against this type of success. A large part of it comes from our outdated, even antagonistic, laws and zoning practices.

Have a Drink

Today's downtowns are hugely influenced by food and beverage establishments, especially those that sell beer, wine and liquor. The United States has had a long and complex relationship with alcohol. In 1933, after thirteen years of Prohibition, the United States repealed the 18th Amendment, which had outlawed alcoholic beverages. The original law, called the Volstead Act, eliminated the sale, production and distribution of alcoholic spirits but interestingly not the consumption of said spirits. It arose out of the so-called temperance movement, which believed alcohol and alcoholism were societal problems that needed to be eliminated, the way one would eliminate polio or the measles. Clearly alcoholism remains a societal problem but this approach—eliminate supply to eliminate the problem—seems very simple-minded in light of what we now know about the nature of addiction.

While the movement was well-meaning, it also had serious effects that ran counter to its intention. John D. Rockefeller, Jr., son of Standard Oil founder John D. Rockefeller and a wealthy supporter of the temperance movement, eventually came to realize that "drinking has generally increased; the speakeasy has replaced the saloon; a vast army of lawbreakers has appeared; many of our best citizens have openly ignored Prohibition; respect for the law has been greatly lessened; and crime has increased to a level never seen before."[ciii] There also emerged a purely economic reason for repeal—tax revenue. Prior to Prohibition, it was estimated that federal, state and local governments generated approximately 14% of their total tax revenue from alcohol commerce.[civ] In the midst of the Great Depression, this revenue was sorely missed.

The 21st Amendment, which repealed Prohibition, turned the governance of alcohol commerce back to the states. In turn, each state created some type of a licensing and administrative board to regulate the trade. Liquor licenses were closely guarded, as a way to limit the perceived negative effects of alcohol and those partaking in alcoholic beverages. Crudely, but succinctly put, citizens did not want drunk people near children in schools. While that may be a public policy point that we can all agree upon today, in practice the limitations alcohol sales and consumption can handicap the very downtowns we are seeking to develop.

Over time, this situation led to a massive patchwork of rules and regulations revolving around the standard notion that alcohol consumption should be limited, based on legitimate public safety and health concerns. To achieve this, governments fell back into the Prohibition mindset that believed the problem was a question of supply. If you limited the supply you could manage the problem, so the solution was to limit the number of establishments that could distribute and sell spirits. Liquor licenses became highly sought after and highly valuable, in effect preventing bars from popping up on every available street corner. Most of our current laws are remainders of this post-Prohibition legacy.

The makers of these laws envisioned a certain type of drinking establishment as their target —namely, bars and restaurants. When these laws were codified, that was the primary retail environment for alcohol sales. Today, you can buy beer and wine in supermarkets, convenience stores, and drug stores in most places. Some states even allow liquor sales in those businesses as well. In the present-day environment, the idea of curbing consumption through limiting bars and restaurants no longer has the same effectiveness. However, we see an echo of this impact in the way that many cities are keen to limit the presence of too many bars and nightclubs to prevent negative economic impact on other businesses in the same area. This type of limitation is based less on public health concerns and more upon throwing local economies and communities out of balance. In my own region, I have seen this very thing happen.

Ybor (pronounced Ee-bor) City is a historical Cuban neighborhood in Tampa, Florida. It was the center of Tampa's cigar production by Cuban immigrants in the early 20th century. In its heyday, Tampa was the world's leading producer of cigars. Following World War II, cigar consumption dropped precipitously, oddly enough because in part, the US military gave cigarettes to all its personnel, thereby changing their smoking preferences. By the 1960s and 70s, the cigar industry had long departed, leaving grand old factory spaces and classic buildings waiting to be redeveloped. In the 1990s, the neighborhood was known as a cheap-rent mecca for artists who set up studios, galleries, and performance spaces. Small business owners and a few bars settled in. In an attempt to further nurture the area's economic development, the city granted several liquor licenses to new club owners, and a burgeoning entertainment district took off. But by the early 2000s, Ybor City was dominated by bars and nightclubs—and the artists and original retail shops were forced out as the nighttime economy took over. The bars and clubs were generating income that fueled rents to rise beyond what non-alcohol-oriented businesses could afford. Over a decade, Ybor City became a one-dimensional economy.

Belatedly, the City of Tampa began a concerted effort to spur more residential and business development in the area. Because of its historic character, Ybor was able to rebound, attracting many businesses in the creative industries such as architecture firms, design shops, video production, and advertising agencies. Residents followed, and Ybor was able to claw its way back to a balance of day and nighttime economies, with multiple roles as a business, residential, and entertainment district. Yet it remains a cautionary tale for any community about the rampant proliferation of liquor licenses.

Today, the types of businesses that are seeking liquor licenses in downtowns is fundamentally different. A local art gallery may do a pottery-making "paint and sip" event, where patrons can enjoy wine with their art. Bike shops may have craft beer on tap after your training ride. As consumers, we want places that have food, coffee, and alcoholic beverages to pair with an experiential opportunity to hang out with our friends. These are hybrid businesses where drinks are part of a creative experience but not the central offering.

Microbreweries and small batch distilleries couldn't be more different from nightclubs. The former is much more artisanal and craft-oriented than other alcohol-based businesses. They need space for creative production, not dance floors, and they create different types of jobs in comparison with nightclubs—yet they fall into the same regulatory scheme. These businesses are bringing together entrepreneurs, craftspeople, and co-creators in a fantastic mash-up of local flavor and local love.

Until I wrote this book, I would not have thought liquor licenses would play such a role, but these licenses clearly play a role in the emotional infrastructure of our places. Too much or too little can dramatically impact the emotional state of people as they interact with their neighborhoods and downtown. Having read my paean to all things alcohol, it might surprise folks to learn that I don't drink. I am half Japanese and have the so-called "Asian flush"—when I drink, I turn bright red. Essentially, I'm allergic to alcohol, so I don't often partake. But I do love what beer, wine, and spirits can bring to a community. They are social lubricants, of course, but as we have seen with the rise of brew culture, micro-vineyards, and micro-distilleries, they are also unique expressions of community character and identity, and in many instances create key destinations for residents of, and visitors to, their cities.

Experiential Retail

I'm a big fan of board games. Not the board games most of us played as kids, e.g., Monopoly and Risk, but contemporary board games such as Settlers of Catan, Dominion, and Ticket to Ride. These more recent board games simulate complex enterprises like making wine, nation building, colonizing Mars or even commanding rebel forces against an evil imperial empire. Due to imaginative new games like these, board games have undergone a major resurgence in the past decade and are once again a big business. The sector grew by 28% in 2017[cv] and has become a $1.4 billion industry.[cvi] Growth is expected to continue to expand into the 2020s.[cvii]

Why, in this digital age, would something as old school and analog as a board game be so appealing? The success of these games seems to be fueled in part by the increasing amount of time we spend with screens. Today, board games allow us to unplug, get immersed in the game, and engage with each other as we sit around the table. They provide a necessary social connection in this highly virtual world. Local game stores typically offer game nights for local patrons, but more and more we are seeing the emergence of a new hybrid of game store, café, and meeting space—the board game café.

Board game cafés provide vast libraries of games, places to sit and play, and offerings of food, coffee drinks, tea—and, increasingly, beer and wine. Many also have a small cover charge to maintain the libraries and pay staff. These cafés are not primarily for kids or even families with children. Their audience is adult, educated, and looking for something that is highly social.

The first board game café in North America is generally regarded as Snakes & Lattes in Toronto, Canada. Founded in 2010, Snakes & Lattes has become the archetypal board game café. Now with three locations in Toronto and employing more than 100 people, it is a destination for locals and travelling game enthusiasts alike. On a typical weekend night, there is a multi-hour wait time for a table. In addition to Snakes & Lattes, there are (as of the publication of this book) more than twenty other board game cafés in the Toronto area.[cviii]

I interviewed Steve Tassie, whose job title at Snakes & Lattes is Curator and Head Game Guru. Tassie has been with the company almost from its beginning. He told me that "board game cafes are the future of retail in the board game industry... something beyond what Amazon can provide." Tassie may be more right than he knows.

According to Grande Prairie, Alberta, Mayor Bill Given, the type of experiential businesses exemplified by board game cafés are the future of downtown retail, period.

I last visited Grande Prairie in late 2016. Mayor Given and I had met a few years earlier, when I led a community workshop in his city. At the time, Grande Prairie was one of the fastest growing cities in Canada, thanks to the booming oil and gas business in the region. By 2016, that sector had stalled, and growth had slowed, but the city remained on a positive trajectory. The mayor was eager to show me some recent developments in the downtown. As we toured the city's core, the mayor pointed out a board game café called Cards. He told me that the café was exactly the type of retail he wanted to see downtown—highly experiential and local. Grande Prairie has a plethora of big box retail stores on its main drag into town. While those stores were huge drivers of the retail economy, Mayor Given felt that the city's downtown needed a different breed of retail to succeed.

"Once we can sell anything online and people are comfortable buying most anything online, the question is: What's left to fill up these downtown spaces? People coming together to do things," Given told me. He pointed out that the local comic book and collectibles store had added a canteen and that, elsewhere, a virtual reality arcade had just opened. These types of experiences, he noted, can't be replaced by shopping on Amazon. A 2014 study conducted in the United Kingdom backs him up. The study concluded that "the 'experiential' touch points of the customer journey—including social interaction, visits to cafes and restaurants, and atmosphere—heighten enjoyment, prolong dwell time, increase spend, and deter consumers from resorting to the online alternative."[cix]

As retail behaviors shift, it is the big box retailers, primarily located outside of city centers, that are most likely to feel the pinch as online sales become easier and more seamless. Some experts suggest that the suburbs will be the losers in this "retail apocalypse."[cx] Distinctive and experiential downtown retail, intermixed with bars, restaurants, residential, and office space, will likely be more resilient to this shift in consumer behavior than suburban malls.

Local Love

Thus far, the downtown resurgence has favored locally owned stores and restaurants, not necessarily because of conscious policy decisions by cities, but a rather simple fact: smaller spaces. Downtown buildings, built in the early 20th century, never envisioned big box retailers and their space requirements. Downtown retail footprints are often ideal for smaller entrepreneurs, many of whom are opening unique operations that add to the local flavor and cultural vitality of their places. Of course, some urban entrepreneurs are opening Subway sandwich shops—and while Subway may fill a much needed food option at a particular price point, it does not add to the local identity of its community. Even a Starbucks, with its great third space sensibility, does little to enhance local identity. These types of businesses do, however, show up on our economic development scorecards, and therein lies one of our major challenges.

In order to track economic progress and success, cities look at several metrics and data points, but the two primary ones that every politician and citizen alike understands are "jobs created" and "tax base." National and international brands, such as Subway and Starbucks, bring a strong record of job creation, payroll taxes, and visibility. When you announce that Starbucks is opening downtown, people instantly recognize the brand and the perceived "win" for the city. Announce that a local coffee shop is opening, and you may have to convince many people of the relative value of the enterprise to the community, simply because they don't know the brand. As a result of these (mis)perceptions, "buy local" and independent business promotion programs have arisen in cities all over North America. These programs are helping to create a cultural and attitudinal shift in their communities, with the result that people are increasingly seeing value and importance in supporting local businesses.

What has impressed me about such programs is how, at first, they used an economic argument: Local businesses re-circulate much more money back into the local community than chains. For retail stores, the percentage was about 50% (local) versus 15-20% (chains). For local restaurants versus national restaurants, it was even more pronounced—more than 70% versus 30%.[cxi] The "local first" movement has not abandoned this compelling economic argument, but many of its champions have moved beyond—into an emotional arena that appeals to residents' sense of local pride and affection, reinforcing the relationship between personal and collective identity, and place. The term "locavore" (sometimes spelled "localvore") appeared over a decade ago and is used to describe people who predominantly eat and shop locally. In fact, the term was selected as the 2007 Word of the Year by the New Oxford American Dictionary.[cxii]

More than 40% of millennial consumers say they prefer to buy from local businesses even if the goods or services are more expensive than mass-market alternatives.[cxiii] A generation ago, consumers at large had no idea what "fair trade" or "farm to table" meant, yet now these terms reflect cultural values that are shaping our economic decisions. More and more of us now state that we desire to feel more connected to the products we are buying, and that by purchasing them from local merchants in our own downtowns and neighborhoods, we are simultaneously feeling more connected to our community. This retail trend goes hand in hand with our overall desire to want to connect with our places and find them distinct, meaningful and, yes, lovable.

Simply put, these programs have made it cool to buy local. This is a remarkable feat considering that it can sometimes mean paying higher prices and forgoing the convenience of a big box retailer or Amazon! Through education, marketing, promotion, and a bit of appeal to our desire to be cool and trendy, the notion of buying local, eating local and yes, drinking local has become a community identifier, especially with younger, more urbane, and more educated community members. Conscious consumerism has made us aware of where and with whom we spend our money, and the appeal of local is clearly persuasive, sometimes even more so than cost and convenience.

Not Your Typical Business

Savvy national companies are also observing the shift in consumer attitudes and coming up with innovative concepts that foreshadow even more changes to come. In late 2017, I visited the lovely community of Delray Beach in South Florida. On Atlantic Avenue, the main street for shopping in downtown Delray Beach, there is a Capital One bank. A bank in a downtown—shocking, I know! But this bank is very different from any other bank I previously experienced.

This Capital One branch is actually a coffee shop and community meeting space, featuring conference rooms with whiteboards, and a few ATMs and automated banking kiosks—but no tellers. Dubbed Capital One Café, it stems from a partnership with Peet's Coffee and looks more like a bright, airy coffee shop than a traditional bank. Laura Simon, the Executive Director of the Downtown Delray Beach development organization, explained to me that there had been some skepticism from city officials about locating the branch in downtown Delray Beach, as it would be taking over a space previously occupied by a popular breakfast café, where locals met and deals were made. But once residents came and experienced the results, they realized it was not just another bank branch.

Capital One Café – Delray Beach, Florida

As of early 2018, there were twenty-five Capital One Cafés in the U.S. with plans for many more. In the spring of 2018, I traveled to Bellevue, Washington, and happened upon another Capital One Café that had just opened. Compared to the one in Delray Beach, this one was vast—7,500 square feet in the heart of Bellevue's downtown business district. What is notable about the space's size is the associated cost of doing business. Downtown Bellevue's central business district includes the most expensive commercial space in the region, even more expensive than downtown Seattle.[cxiv] For a bank to open up such a significant presence, without its most traditional services on offer—I wondered what that portended about the future of the company's business. I spoke with several members of the Capital One launch team that was onsite. They explained that Capital One felt like its cafés reflected the future of consumer banking. Because people can do their banking from virtually anywhere today, the café becomes a way for the bank to connect with its customers and potential customers in a low-key manner. As people sit, enjoy their coffee and have meetings in the space, they are positively associating the experience with this big corporation. So, when they might need some information about a car loan or a business line of credit, Capitol One is already in their headspace. Even banks—the very definition of staid, conservative business—are getting into the experiential realm and developing third spaces!

In downtown Tampa, Florida, a local real estate company purchased a small local coffee shop in September 2016. The company's main goal was not to become a coffee entrepreneur but to create an attractive working space for its agents and employees. Explaining his rationale, Bay to Bay Real Estate owner James Ramos said, "the realtors can have a nice place to work cooperatively, and they appreciate having the foot traffic and accommodations that a restaurant offers."[cxv] Ramos also noted a significant change in working environments that millennial employees are seeking. "One of the strategies for working with millennials in real estate—they work and operate differently than agents who are my age," Ramos said. "They like a more social setting."[cxvi]

Downtowns are the economic, social, and psychic centers of a community. Their decline more than a generation ago was a harbinger of the changing attitudes and culture of the time. It was also a direct result of our ignorance and indifference to the emotional infrastructure that downtowns provide. The current and ongoing resurgence of downtown reflects another swing in the pendulum of changing preferences and, hopefully, a new-found awareness of the emotional value of city centers. What kinds of people and businesses will want to be downtown? What types of activities will they want to do in your downtown? The examples related here are just initial forays into entirely new and unexpected expressions of a desire to rediscover the hearts of our cities. But, with super-exciting changes come super-sized challenges for city leaders. Rules written decades ago are now deployed to govern businesses that haven't existed before, in the midst of technology that changes and evolves at breakneck speeds, with increasing cultural preferences for hybridity and fusion, de- and re-constructing old models, and busting up boundaries. Downtowns—the economic, cultural and psychic centers of our cities—will be the crucible in which experiments like those underway in retail continue to play out.

Peter Kageyama

CHAPTER 5 - RETROFIT THE PAST

Rolling Acres Mall in Akron, Ohio opened in August 1975 to much fanfare. It was the only two-story mall in the region at the time, and it had all the best design amenities of the age: a huge open-air atrium with water fountains, a movie theater, and a food court. During high school in the early 1980s, I worked at the mall's Rite-Aid Drug Store. Rite-Aid certainly wasn't the coolest store—it was no Chess King or Camelot Music—but I had made it into the mall. Rolling Acres was the place to be and would continue to be central to community life until the early 2000s, when changes in demographics, technology, and consumer behavior coalesced into a seismic move away from malls. If you Google "Rolling Acres Mall" today, you will find it prominently featured on several "dead mall" and "retail then-and-now" websites as an exemplar of the genre.

Those of us who are of a certain age all have our Rolling Acres Mall. These sites of former retail glory and other architectural remnants are lingering ghosts of our past. Most are nothing more than footnotes, but some have held places of significance in the stories of our communities. When these historic spaces find a second or third chance and re-emerge in their places with renewed identities, they are potent tonics and beacons for the possibility of a better place. We hold them in a different light, as they represent the past, the present, and the possible future.

When we preserve or re-imagine an older building, we are not just building physical infrastructure. We are building emotional infrastructure. There is a huge emotional context to these physical manifestations of our past. They provide us with opportunities for memory and reflection about who we are as people and as a place. They allow us to claim our past and know more about who we are. Such change can build resilience and determination in us and our places by evincing a willingness to hold onto something, to value something despite its cracks and broken bits. Claiming the past in this way shows that not everything is disposable, and we are not fair-weather friends, or citizens, of a place.

I have written and spoken about Detroit extensively because it has been, and continues to be, a magnificent laboratory for community experiments and a great exemplar to other places. In part, that is because of the heights from which it has fallen, but more so because of the amazing transformations it has manifested in the past decade. A perfect example played out in 2018 with old Michigan Central Station, in Detroit's Corktown neighborhood. The station had been the iconic urban ruin that sat empty and broken for years. It was finally purchased by the Ford Motor Company to be renovated into the centerpiece of a 1.2 million square foot campus, focused interestingly on self-driving vehicles. The once-magnificent building, first opened in 1914, sat empty and grew into a decrepit shell after 1988, when the Amtrak station formerly housed inside shut down. Over the years, the building fell into decay as nature, graffiti artists, taggers, vandals, and scrappers took their pound of flesh from the station. As Detroit slipped into citywide decline, the station became a symbol of the once mighty city's fall. In a famous 2009 *Detroit Free Press* editorial, writer Jeff Gerritt suggested that "demolishing the depot will erase the city's most iconic eyesore, but it won't end the blight on the blocks. Maybe we need this rotting relic to remind us how far we have fallen, and how far we must travel together."[cxvii] From my own first visits to the city over a decade ago, I still have distinct memories of the crumbling station appearing on the horizon as I drove into downtown Detroit. My eye could not help but be drawn to it, and the sight both fascinated and saddened me.

The Moroun family, owners of the Detroit International Bridge Company, bought the property in 1996. Over the next twenty years, there would be talks, negotiations, plans, and false starts for the building. My own friends in Detroit viewed the Moroun family as mostly indifferent to the station and hoped that it would eventually be sold to someone with a vision for rehabilitating the building. On June 11, 2018, after months of rumors and decades of waiting, it was confirmed that the building would be purchased by Ford for $90 million[cxviii] and repurposed as the epicenter of a new industrial campus in the city's Corktown neighborhood. I imagine that the opening of that Ford campus, planned for 2022, will be one of the most celebrated milestones in Detroit history. Reviving Michigan Central Station is more than retrofitting the past, it is *reclaiming* it—raising up the past to new levels to inspire a whole new generation of Detroiters. How fitting it will be that Ford Motor Company is the entity bringing the building back into use. A car company leading the way in the Motor City, as an iconic building rising from the ashes like a magnificent phoenix and finds a new purpose in the 21st century… just thinking about it gives me goose bumps.

The Legacy of Sears

Sears, Roebuck and Company was founded in 1892 in Chicago, Illinois. It began as a mail order catalog business (the e-commerce equivalent of the day!) and did not actually open retail stores until 1925. In the decades that followed, the company rapidly expanded its operations, opening over 3,500 stores worldwide,[cxix] and growing into the world's largest retailer—a title Sears held until 1989, when Walmart eclipsed it.[cxx] In 1974, the company opened the Sears Tower in downtown Chicago, which was the world's tallest building for decades. In its heyday, Sears wielded the commercial power of Amazon and Walmart combined. It was a behemoth.

Today, Sears is shadow of its former self. It seems like only a matter of time before it is relegated to the pages of history, as store closings are the constant stream of company news. In October 2018, the company filed for bankruptcy[cxxi] and in early 2019, the company barely survived liquidation of its assets.[cxxii] I don't highlight this to denigrate Sears, past or present. In fact, it is the rare business that can sustain itself for more than 100 years across three centuries—all credit to Sears. But the retailer's decline has left a staggering amount of infrastructure in communities all over the world, which in turn has caused those communities to ask, "What the heck are we going to do with all this space?"

Peter Kageyama

Atlanta's Ponce City Market

In 1926, as part of their vast retail expansion, Sears opened a massive facility in downtown Atlanta, Georgia. The space occupied more than 2.1 million square feet and included a regional headquarters, a catalog sales distribution center, and a retail storefront. In 1987, Sears sold the facility to the City of Atlanta, which re-imagined it as "City Hall East" for the rapidly growing metropolis. City government moved over 2,000 employees to the site, added a city art gallery, and later incorporated county, state, and federal offices. Even with all that usage, the sheer square footage was just too much for the city to maintain. In 2011, the city sold the property to Jamestown, a private equity firm based in Atlanta. The firm announced that it would create "Ponce City Market," an ambitious new third act for the historic space.

The vision for Ponce City Market, according to managing director Michael Phillips, was to build one of nation's great food halls, on par with Pike Place in Seattle, the Ferry Building in San Francisco and Chelsea Market in New York City, which was also developed by Jamestown.[cxxiii] Phillips described Chelsea Market as a "place where local and artisanal food purveyors could sell their wares" and confirmed that Ponce would follow the same principles. "We are looking to attract the best local, regional, and national restaurants that we believe will thrive in this market."[cxxiv] After much anticipation, the $180 million redevelopment project opened in August 2014. Today, Ponce Market includes an impressive food hall, as promised, as well as lots of local retail, office space, 259 apartments, and a rooftop amusement park. The rooftop is an attraction unto itself. It boasts a miniature golf course, boardwalk-style games, a bar, a special event space (yes, you can get married up there), and some of the best skyline views in Atlanta. The project has been a huge hit with residents, and has been a cornerstone of the revitalization of the Old Fourth Ward neighborhood, together with the amazing Beltline linear park that will encircle downtown Atlanta with twenty-two miles of walkable, bike-able trails when complete. Early work on the Beltline included a section in the Old Fourth Ward, already open to the public and located near Ponce Market, and a new neighborhood park. The synergy in these two major developments resulted in the neighborhood being named one of the 10 best in the country in 2017 by a national real estate organization.[cxxv]

Memphis' Crosstown Concourse

In 1927, just one year after the opening of the Atlanta distribution center, Sears opened a 600,000 square foot Memphis center, around two miles from downtown. On opening day in August, more than 30,000 shoppers showed up to see the new facility. Over the next thirty years, Sears added more and more employees and operations to the location, ultimately expanding the facility to occupy 1.5 million square feet of space. Following the same trajectory as its Atlanta sibling, the Memphis site closed in 1993 and quickly became an empty ruin, a hole in the fabric of its community.

The closing of Sears and the shuttering of the company's building was particularly painful for Memphis. The name of the shopping center, "Crosstown," referenced its location as a central nexus for the entire city. In the 1920s, the City of Memphis had built trolley lines through the neighborhood as an economic development incentive to Sears. (Even a century ago, we were playing that game)! In its heyday, most of the public transportation in the city connected back to the Crosstown area. When Sears declined and eventually closed, its failure was felt across Memphis, but most acutely in the immediate surroundings—which became one of the city's most disadvantaged neighborhoods.

For seventeen years, the building sat empty. Then, in 2010, prompted in part by the nationwide rebirth of older downtowns, attention focused once again on the Crosstown. But initial ideas for the space did not come from the city or the development community. A new vision for the Crosstown came from University of Memphis art history professor Todd

Richardson and local artist Chris Miner. In retrospect, their fresh perspective as outsiders to traditional economic development may have given them a creative edge. Most people in Memphis looked at the vast ruin and could only see its negatives qualities. Many residents wanted simply to see the dangerous space leveled to make way for something new.

In an interview about the project, Richardson explained: "We had to think about 'building' both as a verb and a noun—redeveloping a structure, but at the same time building community."[cxxvi] Richardson and Miner recognized that the size and prominence of the structure created a unique opportunity to create a neighborhood-scale development. They started to call it a "vertical urban village," asking themselves: "What if we took all of these things that really make a vibrant neighborhood and, rather than spreading them out horizontal in a traditional neighborhood way, began to stack them on top of each other?"[cxxvii] Richardson and other supporters of the concept formed the Crosstown Arts Organization, a non-profit with the mission of redeveloping the site. By 2012, they had assembled a small group of local, founding tenants including three healthcare providers—St. Jude Children's Hospital, Methodist Le Bonheur Healthcare and Church Health—who committed, collectively, to leasing some 600,000 square feet of the project. Internal demolition on the building began in 2014, and by 2017 the $200 million project was nearing completion.

Beyond the concrete reality of the reclaimed building, Richardson was also healing a critical wound for his city. The hole left by Crosstown in the city's metaphorical heart and its urban core was something that weighed upon and impacted every Memphian. In my book *Love Where You Live*, I talked about the notion of holes in the fabric of your city and the ongoing emotional damage that these visible and persistent failures, both big and small, create in our cities. The Crosstown hurt more because of its size, its central location, and its visual prominence to every Memphian as they traversed their city. Said Richardson, "there is a price to be paid by the whole city for buildings that are abandoned and left empty." The Crosstown had lost its identity, and its role as a hub and connector for the city. "It lost all of those connections. It lost the people. It lost the transactions. It lost the interactions. It lost the shared experiences and the shared encounters. All of those things that define community," said Richardson. His vision would restore those connections.

In the spring of 2017, I had the privilege of touring the project a few months before its official opening. Frank Ricks, one of the principal architects of Looney, Ricks and Kiss (LRK) in Memphis showed me around the work-in-progress. LRK had been the local project lead, and Ricks was understandably excited about the project. Even months before the official opening, there were office tenants in place, a few working restaurants, and even some residential tenants already occupying spaces. There were soaring open air atriums flooded with natural light. The view from the upper floors was dizzying, as was the stunning realization of the vertical urban village that had once been a hopeful concept. Renamed "Crosstown Concourse," the building is now home to 265 apartments—20% of which are priced as affordable housing, a public charter school, a YMCA, healthcare facilities, restaurants, retail shops, and a 425-seat theater. In 2018, the Congress for New Urbanism recognized Crosstown Concourse with its annual Charter Award. The Crosstown has reclaimed its identity as the crossroads of Memphis and is a central connector in the overall fabric of the city.

The Ponce City Market in Atlanta and the Crosstown Concourse in Memphis are two of the most dramatic revitalizations of former Sears properties, but they not the only ones. In the early 20th century, Sears built ten iconic buildings across the US; these sibling facilities rose and fell with the company. Three of them were demolished, but the rest have had fascinating second lives.

In Minneapolis, Minnesota, and Boston, Massachusetts, two former Sears facilities live on as Midtown Exchange and the Landmark Center, respectively. Each 1.2 million square foot building now houses apartments, office spaces, restaurants, and movie theaters. In Seattle, the former 2.2 million square foot Sears distribution center is now the world headquarters of Starbucks. Each of these projects now resides on the National Registry of Historic Places, which further underscores their importance to the story of their communities.

These redevelopments are inspiring examples of retrofitting the past and finding a second, or even third, act for a building. Spaces such as these are remarkably difficult to redevelop for a litany of reasons. The most obvious one is size—it takes a lot of effort and creativity to fill a million-plus square feet. The extraordinary cost of bringing older buildings up to code, removing asbestos or other harmful materials, performing environmental remediation on the land for former industrial sites—these are sometimes overwhelming expenses and often a deterrent to developers. There are quicker and easier ways to make money! But the rewards for doing rehabilitation projects well are considerable. Sure, profits can be made—but in addition to that, these projects have become anchors for the redevelopment of their respective neighborhoods. When the massive eyesore that sat empty or fallow for years comes back to life in a new and wonderful way, a powerful spell is cast on the neighborhood, and even the city as a whole. Such projects have an unusually strong emotional component that must be considered as part of the overall value these projects bring to their places. The projects described above embody a spirit of determination and resilience, a willingness to hold onto something, to value and not dispose of it for something easier. These capacities are part of the emotional infrastructure of our cities and our selves, and this strength can help carry us through the inevitable tough times.

Developers are often labeled as the bad guys and are an easy target for the anger of city residents. Clearly, some deserve that ire and have earned their reputations as cynics motivated only by money. But the best developers are able to see beyond the financial bottom line and make the case to go after the complex, the unusual, and even the ridiculous projects that transcend mere construction and deserve a place among the ranks we usually reserve for artists, innovators and visionaries.

What To Do With Those Big Boxes?

Not every empty building is going to have a historic legacy and great original design. Most will not. So, what can be done with that ugly, former big box retail space from the 1980s that is now shuttered? There are a lot of these spaces, and more are joining the roster every day as former retail giants like Borders and Toys "R" Us leave gaping vacancies in their wake. Toys "R" Us alone left over 800 storefronts[cxxviii] vacant across the U.S. with their June 2018 closure.[cxxix]

What to do with these blocky, often cheaply made buildings with massive parking lots and suburban surroundings? Tearing them down is one option, but adaptive reuse—more complex, challenging, and potentially more expensive—offers some fascinating opportunities. As a side note, the reuse of an existing building is generally by far the more environmentally friendly, "green" option.

There are some suitors for these big boxes. Ironically, the main one appears to be Amazon, the very company that put many now-defunct retailers out of business. There has been much speculation that Amazon would buy a number of Toys "R" Us facilities as part of their expansion plans for Whole Foods, the upscale grocery store it acquired in 2017. Amazon has also purchased big box venues and former malls as distribution centers. In Cleveland, Amazon converted Randall Park Mall into one of its fulfillment center,[cxxx] and there is speculation that Amazon will purchase Rolling Acres Mall in Akron as another.[cxxxi] (Fingers crossed for that, as I would love to see my childhood mall get a second life.)

Other cities have put their big boxes to more creative use. In McAllen, Texas, a former 123,000 square foot Walmart became the city's new main library in 2011. The award-winning design transformed the space into the largest single floor library in the United States.[cxxxii] In Westland, Michigan, a former Circuit City became the new City Hall. "A new City Hall was going to cost us $15 million for 36,000 square feet," recalled Westland Mayor William Wild. "We purchased this building, and we renovated it, and modernized it for $10 million, and it is 63,000 square feet."[cxxxiii]

Bringing the farm indoors

Urban farming seems like a natural use for many of these big boxes. There are over 40,000 urban farms in the United States producing over $15 billion in annual revenue.[cxxxiv] More and more of those farms are not taking over unused green space but rather going indoors, and thanks to an infusion of venture capital in recent years, a large number of high-tech, vertical farm ventures are remaking agriculture. These vertical farms operate in spaces with much smaller footprints than traditional agriculture. In fact, some of the most successful early operations have been situated in shipping containers.

Since 2013, entrepreneurs in Detroit have taken advantage of a city ordinance that legalized the urban farms that had been popping up across the city for years. Today, researchers estimate that there are more than 1,500 urban farms in Detroit, ranging from local community gardens to large-scale commercial operations. Cross this entrepreneurial trend with the huge surplus of vacant buildings in Detroit—an estimated 78,000 in the city[cxxxv] as of 2014—and you get a recipe for high-tech, vertical farming opportunities. The reclaiming of open spaces and fields, along with formerly vacant buildings, and turning them into productive, active assets has been a key factor in Detroit's renaissance.

Other former shopping centers have seen similarly unusual reincarnations, becoming indoor swimming facilities, public storage, medical centers, office space, fitness centers and even a trampoline park (also in Westland, Michigan). These new businesses often challenge existing city usage codes and require some vision and flexibility on the part of city leadership. Their creators may also have to overcome the general public's lack of enthusiasm or, in some cases, fear and cross-generational hostility, particularly with regards to one burgeoning facet of urban agriculture—cannabis.

The Cannabis Conundrum

As of late 2018, thirty states have legalized medical marijuana, and nine—including the entire West Coast of the U.S.—have fully legalized recreational use. It seems only a matter of time before the U.S. joins Canada with legalized and taxed cannabis. I am not making any judgments, pro or con, regarding the substance itself, but rather have come to accept it as part of the tapestry of challenges and opportunities that cities everywhere are dealing with or will be dealing with soon. It seems inevitable that this emerging industry will collide with existing business, retail and city ordinances, provoking inevitable growing pains.

In Cathedral City, California, near Palm Springs, a cannabis growing business applied for permission to locate in a shopping mall, inside an empty 100,000 square foot former furniture store—just the kind of failed retail space many cities would be thrilled to fill. While growing cannabis is legal in California, cities still have control over where such businesses can locate. The Cathedral City planning commission rejected the business's application. "At some point you have to draw the line, and I draw the line on this one," said commission member Barry Jaquess to his local paper. "To take one of the largest retail spaces in our city and say we're going to allow a cannabis related business in it, I find it alarming."[cxxxvi]

Alarming or not, this type of collision of values seems likely to play out with more and more frequency as cities work to balance their policies on cannabis with the realities of business and economic development. Cathedral City Community Development Director Pat Milos said, "The day of the big box stores is slowly coming to an end, and a lot of cities are going to be faced with that reality."[cxxxvii] This can be a hard change for people to wrap their heads around.

We grow up around a particular building and the business it houses, and we think of the space as one type of thing. I often hear this mindset voiced in the Rust Belt, where residents lament the disappearance of the industries that once made their cities great. Often, this sentiment is expressed by the generation that grew up with and even worked in those industries. These folks (typically, our parents and grandparents) look at the vestigial buildings and, instead of thinking about how to re-imagine the remnants, hold onto a hope—often fruitless—that the buildings will once again hold the same businesses and industry they did decades ago. To change the purpose or function of the building is a tacit acknowledgement that those same businesses and industries are not coming back. This reluctance to change is one of the biggest impediments to adaptive reuse projects like those described above moving forward. Folks fear that they are giving up on their past, and we need to help them move beyond that. With any luck, visionary projects in other communities can help more people see new possibilities.

In my travels over the past few years, I have seen a growing number of such redevelopments, and each is inspiring, creative, and visionary. However, not every community is going to have a giant facility like the Crosstown or even a big box retailer. But most have a former restaurant, a supermarket or a bank.

The Newton in Phoenix

In 1961, restaurateur Jay Newton built the restaurant of his dreams. Located on Camelback Road in the emerging metropolis of Phoenix, Arizona, Beefeaters was a classic, sprawling mid-century destination that included banquet and event rooms in its 18,000 square foot space. Fondly described as a "locally unique postmodern simulacrum of what an old English mansion in the desert might look like,"[cxxxviii] Beefeaters was a longstanding Phoenix institution. Local developer Lorenzo Perez likened it to the Brown Derby of Los Angeles in its heyday. But like the Brown Derby and many other iconic restaurants, changing tastes and trends proved challenging for an old school eatery like Beefeaters. Newton had operated the restaurant for forty years when he decided to retire. Rather than close the place, he offered to give the restaurant to anyone who he felt could effectively manage it. In a unique contest that garnered national attention, Newton asked prospects to write a 400-word essay on what they would do with his restaurant.[cxxxix]

Sadly, no new leader emerged from the contest. In 2001, Newton retired and left the restaurant in the care of his sons, who ran it with declining success until 2006 when it closed. The property sat vacant for six years, until John Kitchell and Lorenzo Perez of Venue Projects acquired it. Their vision for the space was to create a mixed-use homage to the past. The new development would, of course, include a restaurant, but also co-working space, community event space, retail and even a bookstore. Kitchell and Perez managed to recruit local independent bookstore, Changing Hands, to open a second location as part of the project. In 2014, they opened "The Newton" in honor of Jay Newton and the rich history of the site.

When I visited the space in 2018, I was dazzled by its re-imagination of original features like an old dance floor, transformed into modular event space, or the original bar, revived as an eye-catching centerpiece where books and beverages (including beer, wine and cocktails) comingle at Changing Hands Bookstore. Perez artfully describes the store as an "events, programming, community activation company disguised as an independent bookstore." I love the idea of a book bar that invites you to browse with booze.

The Newton – Phoenix, AZ

The main sign outside The Newton invites guests to read, dine, shop, and gather. It is in the "gathering" part that the project has truly succeeded. In 2016 alone, The Newton hosted more than 600 events, necessitating a full-time manager who coordinates events for all tenants in a centralized job. The idea behind a shared events manager is that when one tenant cultivates community by hosting a happening, the result is the creation of more community—and, ultimately, more business—for the entire enclave.

Al!ve in Charlotte, Michigan

Al!ve, spelled with an exclamation point, is "an experience-based destination health park"[cxl] in Charlotte (pronounced Shar-Lot), Michigan, near Lansing. The unique operation includes a fitness center, hospital-run rehabilitation services, a medical spa, a community commercial kitchen, daycare, conference space, and a restaurant. There is a winding indoor walking path that is 1/9th of a mile (about 200 yards) and gets a lot of use, especially in the winter. A local CrossFit gym is a tenant, and outside there is a community garden. Before it was a destination health park, Al!ve was a much more modest grocery store.

Felpausch was a family-owned supermarket chain founded in Hastings, Michigan, in 1933. It operated throughout western and central Michigan for decades until it was purchased by Spartan Stores in 2007.[cxli] During rebranding of the former Felpausch stores, several, including the Charlotte store, were slated for closure.

In late 2007, Hayes Green Beach Memorial Hospital purchased the property with the idea of opening a second regional campus. They began an exhaustive "experience design" process that sought input from employees and local residents regarding their needs, wants, and hopes for the space—for both business and community. Open to the public since December 2011, the result is a wonderful mash-up of health-related services, operated by multiple partners. Today, it is hard to believe the original 45,000 square foot space was once a typical grocery store. Design changes included opening up the facility to much more natural light from windows and skylights; painting the walls warm, vibrant colors; and filling the space with plants. Al!ve is technically a medical center, but it feels radically different from any clinic or doctor's office you have ever visited. It feels bright, natural, healthy, fun, and very much alive.

Al!ve Executive Director Patrick Sustrich told me they have over 200,000 annual visitors to the facility which means they are drawing from far beyond the 9,000+ residents of Charlotte. With additions, the project has grown to nearly 70,000 square feet and has begun to fill the seventeen acres it sits upon with an outdoor pavilion, and an interactive storytelling trail where parents read to their kids. More importantly, Sustrich explained, the project gave Charlotte residents something positive to believe in again. The hospital staff thought they were just building a very cool community health center, which they certainly did—what they were (re)building was the emotional infrastructure of their city, by reclaiming a bit of their past and carrying it into the future.

For Whom the Bell Tolls

Crawfordsville, Indiana, population 16,000, is the county seat for Montgomery County, about 45 minutes northwest of Indianapolis. Like many a county seat, the town has a historic courthouse in the heart of its downtown, the epicenter of county business. This particular courthouse has had an evolution a bit more colorful than most.

Originally built in 1876, the courthouse was topped with an ornate clock tower. During routine maintenance in 1941, a painter discovered that the tower was leaning slightly. With World War II raging abroad, the city opted to not fix the tower and, instead, removed it and melted down the bell for steel to be put toward the war effort. Practical and patriotic folks. This left the building with a truncated top—which to my eye, looked a bit like a unicorn with its horn cut off!

Upon his return from military service, local James Marion Kirtley was dismayed to see the tower missing from the building. Kirtley would go on to become a well-respected local doctor, and his lifelong goal was to see the beloved bell tower restored to the courthouse. In 1996, he founded the Montgomery County Courthouse Clock Tower Committee (a bit of a mouthful, that). Apparently, most of the community did not share his vision, and some thought it was a pipe dream.[cxlii] After Kirtley passed away in 2000, the committee, led onward by Sandy Lofland-Brown, continued to pursue his dream. As downtown Crawfordsville started to gain some attention and love from local businesses and developers, others realized that the restoration of the clock tower would be a highly visible and symbolic project for the city. The committee continued to raise money and, on May 17, 2018, eventually had a replica of the original clock tower installed on top of the courthouse. The unicorn had its horn back!

To my outsider eye, this was a huge win for Crawfordsville—one I am not sure they even fully appreciated. Long-time residents were of course proud of the achievement and very happy with the result, but as I have said about infrastructure, especially emotional infrastructure, its emergent qualities manifest over time. Nearly everyone living in the city today had never known the courthouse with a clock tower. Residents had seen pictures and they knew the story, but entire generations had grown up, lived, and died without the tower. Restoring the clock tower to the heart of their city will send ripples of pride and confidence in their city into future generations. The tower is now the highest point in downtown Crawfordsville, and it is the first thing you see on the horizon as you drive into the city. When I spent a few days with the city in 2018 for a community talk and workshop, the tower was the landmark I used to orient myself visually.

Now, the tower's bell sounds every hour, providing an audible landmark as well. Dr. Kirtley himself had remarked how the original sound of the bell was comforting and like "an old friend."[cxliii] Every hour, even if it registers only on a subconscious level, this piece of emotional infrastructure reminds its citizens that it is here, that downtown is alive, and that the city is whole again.

Banks & Ice Cream – Cleveland, Ohio

At the turn of the 20th century, Cleveland was an industrial giant and the seventh largest city in the United States. Cleveland Trust, one of the region's wealthiest banks, opened its iconic downtown office in 1908. The architectural marvel by George B. Post was the third largest bank building in the country at the time and immediately became one of the most recognized buildings in the city. Its dome and Renaissance inspired façade remain gorgeous examples of grand iconic design.

Cleveland began a long period of decline and disinvestment following World War II. Industry moved out and overseas. Like many cities, Cleveland hollowed out to its surrounding suburbs and the once great downtown fell on hard times. In my second book, *Love Where You Live*, I wrote about the ache of the 1995 decision by Cleveland Browns owner Art Modell to relocate the team to Baltimore. Around the same time, Cleveland Trust was acquired by Key Bank, and its offices were moved to a more modern downtown high rise. The Trust Building was shuttered in 1996 and remained mostly closed to the public until 2005. These were tough times in the city.

In 2005, Cuyahoga County purchased the property, but struggled to do anything with it for seven years. Empty and fallow, the site became one of those holes in the fabric of the community that are painful reminders of a better time. In 2012, the county sold the property and its adjacent tower at a loss to Geis Construction from Streetsboro, Ohio. Geis transformed the tower into a boutique hotel, and the Trust Building into a downtown grocery store with office spaces in its upper floors and a nightclub in the basement vault. The grocery store is run by Heinens, the oldest family-owned grocery chain in the Cleveland area. The store is easily the most interesting grocery I have ever seen in the United States. The centerpiece is the gorgeous four-story dome that acts as food court, wine bar, and art gallery to lunch and dinner crowds of businesspeople, downtown residents, and visitors alike.

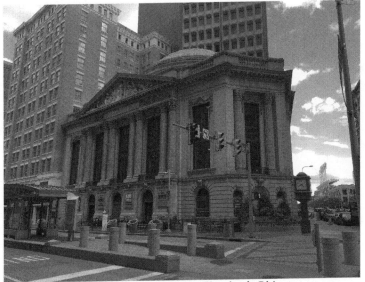

Heinen's Supermarket – Cleveland, Ohio

Just across the Cuyahoga River in the Ohio City neighborhood, you will find some of Cleveland's most beloved businesses and institutions. The West Side Public Market has been operating in the neighborhood for over 100 years. The neighborhood contains the highest concentration of breweries in the entire city, and on West 25th Street you will find some of the best and oldest, including Great Lakes Brewery and Market Garden Brewery. It is a fantastic neighborhood that has become a highly desirable location. In the heart of West 25th Street stands the old Rialto Theater.

The Rialto Theater opened in 1919 and remained one of the city's largest movie and vaudeville venues for years. Like most inner-city theaters, the Rialto lost audiences to the suburban multiplexes and eventually closed in 2005. In 2011 the property was purchased by Pete and Mike Mitchell of Mitchell's Ice Cream, They transformed the theater into an ice cream production facility and corporate headquarters with a retail storefront as well as open gallery spaces where you can watch ice cream being made. The first time you walk into this space, you cannot help but smile and say "wow" because it is so wonderfully unexpected to find ice cream being made inside a historic theater.

There is a concept called "functional fixedness" which describes our mental habit of seeing things in a limited light. For example, when we look at a parking space, we see only a place for cars. We don't see a space for a micro-park or a canvas for a mural. When we look at a theater, we tend to only see a space for performance on a stage. As I travel, I have seen many theater restoration projects and almost all of them are some new variation on a theater. One such building in Liberty, New York, has been converted to a meeting and banquet facility, which is certainly different from a performance space, but still conceptually similar in many ways. In contrast, making a theater into an ice cream factory is remarkable. By the same token, functional fixedness would seem to lead us to see a factory as just a factory, or a store as just a store. That mindset can lead us to build things that meet only the minimal, expected characteristics of a given project but miss out on including unexpected elements that may add up to something special—a "love note" to visitors, if you will.

Mitchell's could have turned the theater into an ordinary factory with corporate offices, but they went beyond to include glass walls and viewing galleries where people can watch the making process behind their product. They offer community rooms that locals can reserve for special events. They went the extra mile to make the entire operation a "green" business that preserved the original features of the building but showcases the latest sustainable technologies and practices in its industry. Mike Mitchell, one of the founding Mitchell Brothers, said of their shops, that they are "not just ice cream shops; we are creating places in the lives of people."[cxliv]

As we look for opportunities to retrofit our past, one hurdle we need to overcome is the (often unconscious) functional fixedness that limits our possibilities. Projects like the ones described above and hundreds more like them, are providing inspiring examples that will serve to help us look beyond our blinders and preconceived notions and to see our cities in a different light.

Every building, every space tells a story. Our sense of place is the amalgamation and internalization of those stories. Some stories are more memorable than others, while some barely register with us at all. New stories catch our attention because we are all attuned to look for the new and novel, and we reward the latest trends with our time, our money, and our attention. A mentality of focusing on the new can lead to steamrolling our past. Here is where the historians and historic preservationists in our communities raise the flag and remind us of the value of our history. It is finding the balance between these two poles that often leads to confrontations between the developers and the historic preservationists. Eventually communities settle into their new equilibrium.

The examples of retrofitting our past in this chapter represent the best of both worlds. Each of these projects takes a community loss—the loss of a business, an iconic building, loss of identity or sense of purpose—and transforms it into a new and unexpected reality, rising from the ashes of history. Such projects are especially important to the psyche and emotional wellbeing of their places because they validate the significance of the past and point to a future of creativity and innovation. These projects challenge both sides—champions of new and old—to compromise and to see beyond their own viewpoint. In doing so, they strengthen the mission of each side and create a whole larger than the sum of its parts. That may be a critical lesson for our times: In compromise, we may not get exactly what we thought we wanted, but we might get something more than we could have imagined alone.

CHAPTER 6 – NEXT GENERATION THIRD SPACES

Sociologist Ray Oldenburg is the godfather of the "third place." In his canonical 1989 book, *The Great Good Place*, Oldenburg gave a name to the idea of the places where we occur beyond home ("first place") and work ("second place"). These third places are public and designed to encourage lingering, people-watching, and socialization. Libraries, public parks, churches and, of course, coffee shops are prime examples of the concept.

Third places had already existed for centuries, but Oldenburg framed the concept in a way that brought it into the mainstream consciousness of businesses and cities everywhere. I had the great pleasure of meeting Oldenburg a few years ago when he visited my hometown of St. Petersburg, and the experience remains a professional highlight for me. We talked at length over dinner about how third places bring all manner of value to communities—including, I noted, inspiring and facilitating greater emotional connection to our cities.

Business and development communities were among the first to fully embrace Oldenburg's ideas. In fact the business community, most notably in the form of Seattle coffee company Starbucks, led the charge over the past 25 years. In 1989, the nascent Starbucks empire consisted of a mere 55 stores.[cxlv] As of summer 2018, more than 28,000 Starbucks coffee shops span the globe. Starbucks represents the quintessential third place for many people. (Though, interestingly, Oldenburg declined to endorse the company when once asked.[cxlvi]) Were Starbucks merely peddling expensive coffee, it would not be the global phenomenon it is today. Starbucks created a whole new category of experience for many Americans, and it redefined coffee culture in geographical areas that had long standing cultures of coffee houses, such as Europe and Oceania.

The coffee shop became a model of what a third place could be and it opened consumers' eyes to something beyond home and work. Commercial and residential developers responded with new ideas of mixed use and town squares that incorporated this emergent desire. The development community, especially the New Urbanists, believe that third places form the social center of a community. They even suggest that such infrastructure be initially subsidized by the developer if necessary. Mapping and then meeting consumer desires is of course what developers and entrepreneurs do. But beyond the market opportunities represented here, the third place offered an insight into how we, as a community of social animals, want to co-exist with each other.

Beyond good business and necessary infrastructure, I would go further and say that these third places should be considered essential emotional infrastructure. We need to be comfortable, happy, and even cozy in our cities. Our technical and engineering-based approaches to city building have led to some less than comfortable results. Hard-edged, impersonal, and brutalist structures are antithetical to our emotional wellbeing. The standard offering of municipal third space—parks, playgrounds, community centers, and the plaza outside City Hall—need to be re-evaluated and expanded upon. Private businesses and organizations have elevated third place design to exciting new levels, which raises the bar and the stakes for cities as they develop much needed and essential civic places.

Consider most peoples' go-to exemplar of a third place—a coffee shop, probably a Starbucks or some locally inspired version of the neighborhood coffee shop. Designed for comfort, conversation and commerce, these are laudable goals for any space (though when they fail as did Starbucks in 2018 in Philadelphia for racially profiling African American customers waiting for a meeting, that failure and resultant backlash are even more stark and telling). When we then compare our experience of that third space with the other environments in our lives, the shortcomings in design and purpose become highly evident. The well-designed coffee shop has put pressure on your other environments, and you did not even know it. Today, we are seeing an emergent crop of dynamic third places that are setting new standards and expectations for design in the civic realm.

Corporate Third Places

It seems odd to say "corporate third place," because the very idea of the third place was something between home and work. Yet in the present moment, when our work lives dominate our available time and consciousness, it is not surprising that businesses have realized the need to redesign workspaces to accommodate expectations beyond sheer functionality and efficiency. This interest is not based in altruism, but rather on a calculated approach to maximizing performance, recruitment, and retention of employees who increasingly expect more from their work environments. Some may see this interest as cynical and self-serving on the part of employers, but I see it simply as an implicit recognition of changing lifestyles and values.

Target, the second largest U.S. retailer behind Walmart, is headquartered in Minneapolis, Minnesota. The company houses more than 8,000 employees[cxlvii] in multiple buildings in the Nicolett Mall area of downtown Minneapolis. In October 2012, Target opened Plaza Commons, a 25,000 square foot "wellness, business, and recreation center"[cxlviii] for employees, in a beautifully refurbished 1920s building. The space resembles an iconic downtown city club with food service, a bar, comfortable seating, meeting spaces, locker rooms, a basketball court, bike storage, and video game rooms. The outdoor space of the commons allows for events and activities such as bocce during summer months and a fire pit during the winter. The Commons has become a de facto student union for Target's downtown corporate campus. Consider how central the student union is to the college experience; classrooms may be where the core learning occurs, but the union is where the experience of student life occurs. Now consider the significance of the Plaza Commons to the quality of their work experience for Target's employees.

"It really is an inspiring, great place where people can come and be their personal best,"[cxlix] said Jodee Kozlak, Target Executive Vice President of Human Resources. Target recognized that healthy, happy employees are good for business. As a corporation, Target brought the idea of great design for all to the forefront of their marketing and branding. It is telling that they are also willing to invest in great spatial design because they recognize a tangible return on that investment.

Ray Oldenberg has observed that, "Corporations used to believe that the longer they could keep each employee at the desk, the more productive they'd be. That's just been shot to pieces. Managers found out that if they let people work where they want and when they want, productivity went up."[cl] Freedom from a desk or workstation, has proved to be foundational in the modern, innovation and creative-based workplace.

Amazon, based in downtown Seattle, Washington, has taken this idea to an even greater extreme. In January 2018, the company opened The Spheres, a cluster of three geodesic domes housing a kind of urban greenhouse. The domes comprise nearly 10,000 square feet and contain more than 40,000 plants between them. At its highest point, The Spheres is over four stories tall; its most majestic residents include a 49-year old giant fig tree. Rather than a greenhouse, the structure is a corporate meeting facility and place to "feel differently, to think differently," said Ron Gagliardo, The Spheres' lead horticulturist.[cli] The Spheres can host 800 employees at a time in a variety of spaces, including a treehouse-like nook in the upper canopy of the facility. The space is reserved for Amazon employees, though the company does offer limited public tours of the facility.

In 2018, I visited Seattle on other business and wanted, like many tourists, to see The Spheres in person. I walked around the structure with the same look of wonder and amusement on my face that I imagine most people get in front of this highly unlikely and disruptive visual element in the heart of downtown Seattle. I stumbled upon the employee entrance and was politely but firmly told there was no public access. But the door was open long enough for me to take in the soaring wall of living plants and the green canopy above. More than the sights, I immediately noticed the rich, warm air and lush smell of plant life. Suddenly, I could imagine how sitting in that fecund, highly oxygenated atmosphere for a couple of hours would be incredibly refreshing. A brainstorming session there would be amazing!

Technically, The Spheres is still a workplace—but a workplace so radically different from the typical corporate office that it might as well be on another planet. Amazon has described The Spheres as a recruiting tool. Of their major tech industry competitors (i.e., Apple, Google, Microsoft), Amazon is the only one with a central urban campus (though we will explore this notion in light of HQ2 in Chapter 9).

Amazon Spheres – Seattle, Washington

The Spheres offer another potential perk that no other competitor can match (yet). It is an investment in Amazon's employees as well as an investment in the neighborhood. Amazon has declined to say how much The Spheres cost to build, but King County has estimated the cost of the project at $284 million.[clii] Granted, Amazon can afford such amenities where many other entities cannot, but as more publicly traded companies (with Amazon and Target at the lead) invest in boundary pushing, expectation raising third places, other companies—and other cities—will need to take notice.

While both the Target and Amazon spaces are exclusive to their employees, the hotel industry is opening itself up to the public by redesigning and rethinking their lobbies as public third places. In 2009, the Ace Hotel in New York City opened. They did not intend it, but their fun and funky lobby became a de-facto co-working space when many of the locals came for the vibe and free wi-fi. The hotel recognized that they were onto something, so they enhanced the public aspect of the lobby to include ubiquitous power outlets and made it known that the space and wi-fi was not just for guests, but for the general public. "What we wanted was for our lobbies to act as community gathering spaces and designed them with that in mind," Kelly Sawdon, partner and Chief Creative Officer at Ace Hotels, said. "Our hotels are borne from our love for cities and people, and that means providing space for everyone, regardless of whether they're guests or our neighbors."[cliii]

Other major hoteliers are following suit. Marriott's Moxy brand emphasizes the communal aspect of their spaces. They proudly declare that "Our lobbies are like living rooms with a bartender."[cliv] Marriott has over 80 Moxy properties in development in the U.S., Europe and Asia. These spaces are catering to the business traveler, often the solo business traveler who, according to Toni Stoeckl, Global Brand Leader and Vice President for Distinctive Select Brand at Marriott, said "Even if you're alone, you want to be alone together, ideally making connections with locals that are actually hanging out in that public space."[clv] In Amsterdam, a new hybrid has emerged – the apartment/hotel/co-working space called Zoku. Described by co-founder Hans Meyer, as "a new category in the hotel industry... a hybrid between a home and office with hotel services," Zoku targets the creative business traveler who is looking for something more than just a hotel room, a bar, and a fitness center. All of these projects portend a shift in the attitudes and desires of workers and employers beyond mere base functionality. They elevate workspaces into experiences that blend social, technological and financial considerations into exciting new possibilities. How municipal entities respond to this changing expectation will proved to be a critical aspect for their long-term economic development strategies and talent attraction and retention efforts.

Civic Third Places

Not far from Seattle in Kenmore, Washington, is a great example of a next generation municipal third place. Kenmore is a small city of 22,000 residents and sits on the northern end of Lake Washington. I visited there for the first time in 2015. At that time, Mayor David Baker and City Manager Rob Karlinsey showed me an ambitious plan to remake their town center.

Kenmore has no traditional downtown, but the city recognized the need for a central gathering space, or what I would call an emotional or "psychic center." Adjacent to their City Hall sat a large surface parking lot with a small, rather dated café located on it. Baker and Karlinsey shared their vision for a revamped town square that would include a unique community center, a public park, and a restaurant adjacent to City Hall.

The Hangar – Kenmore, Washington

In the fall of 2017, Kenmore opened The Hangar, a $4.5 million, 4,650 square foot community space described as a community living room. Inspired by Kenmore's regional sea plane service, Kenmore Air, the space echoes the typical architecture of an airplane hangar. Massive glass doors open out onto an outdoor park, providing sweeping views and lots of fresh air. A coffee shop, wine bar, and conference room are all available for public use. During the day, community meetings take place, students come in to do their homework and the space buzzes like a giant coffee shop. By evening, The Hangar hosts performances, public meetings, movie nights, Seahawk watch parties, and even board game nights. A planned Phase 2 of the development includes a sit-down restaurant on the other side of the park.

The project goes well beyond the typical vision for a community center and reflects the aspiration of the community. Mayor Baker told me, "The Hanger has exceeded my wildest expectations... becoming a major gathering spot... and a love note for our city." He also noted that people are finding new, and sometimes unexpected, uses for the space. He noted that insurance agents have set up meetings in The Hangar right beside high school students doing their homework. "It's hard to tell what The Hanger will become, because it's increasing in popularity almost daily."

Tauranga is a city of 140,000 on the north island of New Zealand. I wrote about the city in *Love Where You Live,* where I highlighted a fantastic public art project called Hairy Maclary Park. My most recent visit showed even more progress in their city center. Tauranga is in the process of tearing down several older municipal buildings and redeveloping them into modern, multi-use facilities that will serve the city for the next generation. However, one downside of the process is that lengthy construction times and limited resources have prioritized certain lots over others. This means some of the lots sat empty as others were redeveloped. As I have noted in the past, an empty lot sends a negative psychological message to residents and visitors alike. The city addressed this issue with a project that was inspired by another New Zealand project called Re:Start Mall in Christchurch.

Re:Start Market is a retail establishment in the heart of downtown Christchurch made up of shipping containers. Re:Start was one of the first things to be opened in the central business district of Christchurch following the earthquake of 2011 that devastated much of the city. The idea behind it was to quickly get something up and functioning to remind people that the city center was still open for business. The shipping containers made for an ideal size for local businesses and Re:Start was a huge success with locals and tourists alike and was hailed for its creative design. It was always intended as a place holder for the central business district and in January 2018, Re:Start was officially closed. Tauranga took the core idea of Re:Start when they began to redevelop their city center.

On one of the key empty lots, they created their version of the container mall called Our Place.

Our Place opened in August 2018 as a temporary project that included not just local retail, but also space for social enterprises, start-ups, performances, and community usage. All this was done with just a couple dozen shipping containers. Said Tauranga City Councilman Larry Baldock, "There is a lot of change happening in our city centre and Our Place is a space that offers a transitional example of where we want to be heading, with plenty of community involvement and activity, and a great space to connect with others,"[clvi]

What I think is brilliant about this project is that in its own microcosm it is modeling the mix of entities that a successful downtown needs to have. It is a tiny village that incorporates the necessary economic, social and cultural elements that make for successful communities. The fact that the city understands the need for a "transitional example" and has embraced this temporary opportunity portends good things for them moving forwards. For one thing, this is a civic experiment that they can learn from. Many of these initial businesses are testing the waters of the city center and may become permanent residents once the project sunsets. The city has created a fantastic third place for residents that is also a business incubator and archetype for future development.

In my last book, I chided (somewhat gently) my hometown of St. Petersburg, Florida for a then-stalled downtown development project, The Pier. Our municipal pier was crumbling and after several years of contentious public input, a voter referendum, and several million dollars in expenses, we found ourselves back at square one; with no pier and no plan. At that time I called this a "self-inflicted wound" and noted with dismay that as of 2015, no meaningful progress was being made on The Pier. Today I am happy to report that the new Pier is in full development and scheduled to open in early 2020. Mayor Rick Kriseman, elected in part due to a prior referendum on the earlier Pier project, has led the charge and demanded that the final project be a world-class destination. In fact, he has successfully lobbied for additional funding of the project. The original budget for the project was $50 million but as of 2019 that number had ballooned to $80 million[clvii]. The project now included a $1 million children's playground along with public art estimated to cost over $2 million. These are all part of the "enhancements" the mayor believes are necessary to create a world-class destination.

The Pier is an example of this next generation of third places in that it had to be far more than the sum of its parts and its official function as a waterfront park. Of course, it had to include some retail, a restaurant, play spaces for kids, boat docks/slips, and a performance space. That kind of design has become standard in large scale public places. Where The Pier distinguishes itself as next generation emotional infrastructure is in the fact that it had to overcome years of doubt and a chorus of naysayers. It could not simply be a functional park or a pier. It had to seal a very large community breach that had divided many people in my community. It had to be a beacon and visible example of the new St. Petersburg that was no longer a retirement destination, known at one point as "God's Waiting Room." It had to be the epicenter of the downtown and *the* community gathering space. It had to be a symbol of youth and vitality, and the city moving in a positive direction. Simply put, it had to be a homerun. Mayor Kriseman told me, "Great cities build great things and create sacred spaces, and when they do, the conversations that follow are never about the cost of materials or construction timelines. They are about the soul of a city."

The mayor and the city have done a great service to our community that many will not fully realize in the short term and may not ever fully apprehend because they don't see the world beyond a financial model. The Pier has a cost, and it's a pretty large one. Those who see the world through that financial lens will always see the price tag. Those of us who are open and willing to see beyond the immediate, the financial, and the obvious will come to understand that the city has created a visible and dynamic "heart" that will shape the perceptions of locals and visitors alike for generations to come. Mayor Kriseman has called it an "integral part of the emotional experience in St. Pete for residents and visitors alike." I cannot emphasize enough how difficult and rare it is that we can actually do that in our places. The psychic and emotional centers of our places are often well-established. Our job, as people who care about a place, is to maintain and perhaps incrementally enhance those centers. When Mayor Dyer of Orlando committed to repairing and modernizing the Lake Eola fountain, he was building emotional infrastructure. The Pier is also emotional infrastructure with a much higher cost, but it is also going to be NEW infrastructure. When the old municipal pier was located in the heart of our downtown, locals saw it as an outdated, kitschy tourist destination. Everyone recognized the old inverted pyramid design, but few of us were actually proud of that relic. It was not a place that drew our presence, our money, or our love. The expectation of the new Pier is that it will be our Central Park – a place that not only enhances our downtown, but provides an overarching monument to the aspiration of our community.

City leaders and urban planners have long recognized the concept of the third place, but they have often been reluctant to make concrete investments in it for fear of spending public dollars on something others may see as frivolous and then being called out publically in the local editorial column. Now city leaders are using corporate examples like those above to pave the way for civic investments in similarly innovative design. Their impact is being seen on civic projects that stretch beyond their most immediate and obvious needs and provide a new benchmark in our thinking on infrastructure. There will always be naysayers who look at any investment beyond mere functionality as wasted money. Let us not limit ourselves and our vision for our cities to that of our most parsimonious citizens. Those folks simply may not be able to imagine something new and different beyond their own experience. Such a limit may seem financially sound—wise, even, in times of budgetary challenges—but a city that merely does what is expected, in the most cost-effective manner possible, is at best on a long-term trajectory to mediocrity. This is most likely a formula for failure as other places, making investments in beauty, art, great design, and emotional infrastructure, will find the successes of their projects (and even their failures) building upon each other and creating that "great, good place" that people flock to, protect, and love more than any other.

CHAPTER 7 – EMOTIONAL PLACEMAKING: "ROSES & THORNS"

In the summer of 2017, I spoke to a group of interns from the Kauffman Foundation in Kansas City, Missouri. After reading my books, they had searched for small, inexpensive projects to inspire love in their city. One of their ideas was the simple gesture of giving out flowers (roses, actually) to people in public places. They tested out the idea to see how people would react. Generally speaking, people were very pleasantly surprised and appreciated the gesture. What surprised them the most, the interns told me, was that the biggest reactions, both positive and negative, occurred at the city's bus station. They recounted that folks at the bus station were moved in a positive way more so than at any other location. They also recalled one woman who declined the rose, saying that she did not like Kansas City. Rejection!

I told the group that I wasn't surprised by the

responsiveness of the bus station crowd. Sadly, I believe, most people at a bus station aren't expecting to see something beautiful—so when presented with a rose, they are that much more surprised and moved. The opposite reaction, represented by the woman who turned down the rose, may have been made more extreme by taking place at the bus station. Recall the bluntness of the woman's comment about not liking Kansas City. I'm just conjecturing, but it wouldn't surprise me if she had had a bad experience with the city's transportation system. If so, her reaction was a negative emotional response to one of the city's critical design elements—and the sign of a failure of its emotional infrastructure.

Let's be honest. Public transportation, particularly in the United States, is a class issue. While not exclusively so, public transportation, especially bus service, is the primary option for large portions of the poor and working classes. While transit hubs like bus stations may be functional, efficient and safe (at best), they are much less likely to be beautiful, well-designed, and inspiring places. *The Happy City* author Charles Montgomery noted in his book that "administrators typically choose the most utilitarian-looking materials for bus interiors and stations—even when attractive finishes are no more expensive—simply to avoid the appearance of having wasted money. The result are systems that repel wealthier commuters and depress those who have little choice."[clviii]

The exception that proves the rule opened in August 2018 in San Francisco. The three-block long Salesforce Transit Center is both a bus depot and a five-acre public park. The facility is a gorgeous architectural marvel that cost $2.2 billion dollars and took eight years to build. One of the more remarkable features is that the park is on top of the transit center. By 2029, regional train service will be added to the depot, but for now it offers only bus service. Designed by internationally renowned Pelli Clarke Pelli Architects, the structure was described by one commentator as "an exceedingly rare species: the bus-station-as-Instagram-backdrop."[clix]

Why would San Francisco build such a beautiful bus station? The answer can be found, in part, in the name. The headquarters of Salesforce, the corporate software giant, stand right next to the center, and the company paid a reported $110 million for naming rights to the station.[clx] The station itself, and the dazzling park above, are recruitment and productivity tools for Salesforce, not unlike Amazon's Spheres in downtown Seattle. Transportation is a critical issue for the San Francisco Bay area, and companies like Salesforce know that their workforce needs options other than the personal automobile. San Francisco represents an extreme case of the challenges that explosive urbanization and development pose to cities, so it is not surprising that they would be leading in this arena. Cities had been able to under-invest in their public transportation systems for decades because poor residents were the primary people using public transit. In our most rapidly urbanizing cities, this is no longer the case. When high-tech, highly educated workers are choosing to use public transportation, then we build better bus stations.

It is a sad state of affairs when our actions suggest that we believe some people are less deserving of beauty and great design than others. I imagine the woman in Kansas City who turned down the rose, exposed to such indifference repeatedly over time, has come to believe that her city does not care about her. I don't believe that the designers of the bus station in Kansas City are classist, but I do believe that they had not been challenged to think about the emotional impact of their work on the people the bus station was designed to serve. They were tasked with making it functional, safe, aesthetically appealing (enough), and completed on time and on budget. Had they been asked to consider long-term emotional effects, I suspect the end result might have been different—perhaps more like the Salesforce Transit Center in San Francisco. Had they been tasked with the mission of creating an emotionally equitable design, I believe the results would have been even better.

Cities must be recognized as a complex stew of people, transactions, encounters, and emotions. To discount or dismiss the emotional context of places gives us, at best, a partial understanding of that place and, at worst, renders us tone-deaf idiots careening from mistake to mistake as we engage with our places. With a better emotional understanding, we are better able to understand complex problems, such as gentrification or income inequality, in new and more nuanced ways. We begin to realize that emotional states are metaphorical bridges that we can build or tear down as we would a building. This awareness of emotional infrastructure then prompts the question: What emotions do you want to promote or negate in your place?

Generally we would all agree that love is a good thing. However, love is also ephemeral and personal, and I think it is difficult to translate love into a specific goal. As I have noted in my prior books, working toward a lovable city is about creating a set of conditions through which the desired emotional response (i.e., love) *might* occur. Love is not a formula; it is a far more complex emotion than most and, some would say, a state of being. I believe that love, in this civic sense, is the cumulative effect of many interactions, big and small, some intentional and many accidental, coming together to create that most amazing of feelings. Some of the emotions outlined below flow into that end state and are key determinants of whether the conditions for love emerge.

In the introduction to this book, I pointed out that some of the most typical responses from citizens about their cities are predictable and common across the developed world. I said that, if asked about their cities, many people will complain about parking, potholes and rents being too high. There are obvious financial and even safety issues to these elements but there is also an emotional story behind each of these complaints. Often, in urban planning, city government and economic development, we are not addressing the underlying feelings but instead are treating symptoms—not the truly fundamental issues. Perhaps the most important element in this mix is one that continues to elude us. Despite rising awareness and sensitivity, evidence suggests that this element is getting worse. That element is equity or, more simply put: fairness.

Why Fair Is Crucial

Human beings are social animals. We live together, work together and need each other, not just to survive but to thrive. We believe in the idea of equality of all people, but we also recognize that not everyone gets the same house, car, or phone. And, broadly speaking, we are OK with that. As a tribe, as a pack of highly integrated social animals, we recognize that we may not get the first bite of the metaphorical kill, or the biggest portion, but as long as we get something, we're good with that. Experiments with dogs, also highly social animals, yield telling evidence of this. During a series of experiments, some dogs were continually given treats, and some dogs were given nothing. After a while, the dogs who were given nothing walked away from the interaction. When the experiment was repeated and, this time, some dogs were given steak, or another high value treat, and the other dogs got something very basic like kibble, all the dogs stayed engaged. The dogs had no sense of proportion, but they did have a well-established general sense of fairness. Human beings do have a sense of proportion and our fundamental concepts of fairness are being challenged in our communities like never before.

In a time when we very visibly see increasing gaps between the "haves" and "have nots" in our society, the notion of fairness comes even more to the forefront. Author Richard Florida astutely diagrams the extreme effects of what he calls "winner take all urbanism" in his 2017 book, *The New Urban Crisis: How Our Cities Are Increasing Inequality, Deepening Segregation, And Failing The Middle-Class – And What We Can Do About It*, Florida highlights how a select group of "superstar" cities have seen explosive economic growth over the last two decades that far outpaces their nearest competitors. Tech hubs such as San Francisco, Seattle, Austin, Boston, and New York City were the poster children for his "creative class" theories, which posited (correctly) that educated, tech savvy workers would congregate in places that offered the highest wages, urban amenities, progressive social attitudes, and transportation options beyond the car. What Florida came to realize was that "winner-take-all urbanism creates a new kind of inequality between cities, with the economic gulf growing wider and wider between the winners and the losers."[clxi]

Though economic growth is generally a good thing, explosive growth is not without its drawbacks. Housing prices in these super-successful cities have skyrocketed and placed home ownership in doubt for many in those communities. Gentrification (or fears of gentrification) in long-established neighborhoods has radically changed the culture of these cities. Economic homogenization has turned previously diverse, multicultural neighborhoods into monocultures where the key to admittance is tech savviness and creative skill, as valued in the 21st century economy. While this problem is particularly pronounced in so-called superstar cities, it is playing out in cities all over the developed world. As talented people cluster in cities, their economic impact is maximized and reinvested back into their communities as wages, investments, and consumer capitalism. Parts of cities become "hot," while others see disinvestment and neglect. If you are on the right side of the economic equation, you see this change as progress. If you don't have the skills and education to take advantage of the new economy, the city becomes less and less for you. The lion's share of beauty, art, great design—and even fun—seems to belong to the privileged "creative class" (as Richard Florida named this group in his seminal 2002 book, *The Rise of the Creative Class*). And this feels unfair.

In 2011, the Occupy Wall Street movement gave a voice and a name to this sentiment—the "1%" and the "99%" came into our cultural lexicon. But we had yet to make the connection that our cities themselves were amplifying inequity. Our consumer culture makes us desire the latest cell phone. If we can't have it, we feel left out. What is happening across our cities is this feeling of being left out, excluded, and on the losing side of an economic game that plays out on a daily basis with our fellow citizens. This is one of the great "wicked" problems of our age, and there's no single magic bullet that will solve it.

The Good Part of Town

I recently had the experience of being on the receiving end of an innocent comment, made in passing, that has caused me to stop and rethink my fundamental beliefs about cities. I was picking up a prescription for one of my dogs (dog parent here, remember), and I was asked by the cashier to verify my street address. I recited the address for her, and she replied, "Ahh...downtown St. Pete, the good part of town." She was merely making small talk, and the comment was probably part observation and part compliment. Either way, I left there with that phrase rattling around in my head: "the good part of town."

I recognize that downtown St. Petersburg, like many downtowns across the U.S. and the world, has become a desirable place to live. Urban amenities, walkability, and many other factors are fueling the renaissance we see in our downtowns. These places are indeed "good," but they are also becoming more and more expensive—too expensive for many of the city's residents to live there. As we have discussed in previous chapters relating to gentrification and social equity, this growing economic divide becomes a flashpoint for social rifts, creating the sense of "us" versus "them." Downtowns and other expensive neighborhoods cannot be the only places that are "good" for our citizens to call home. If that is the case, we have utterly failed as place-makers, citizens and civic leaders.

Not every neighborhood will be "nice" by empirical standards of beauty, amenities or economic value. They will not all have beautifully landscaped boulevards. They will not all have modern parks, the newest community center or the showcase public library. There will be a range, perhaps even a wide range, in terms of the qualities of each neighborhood in a city. However each and every one of them needs to have something that residents and visitors alike can point to as worthy of respect and value. Just as we (I hope) ascribe value and dignity to all human life—be it rich, poor, homeless or landed—we need to locate a similar baseline for our places.

I often talk about how every successful community needs to be, on a basic level, functional and safe. Some cities struggle to provide even this modicum of service and stability to their citizens. Many would point to the troubles in Chicago's South Side and say the city is failing at these most basic of criteria in that neighborhood—and they would not be wrong. The murder rate in the South Side is shocking and, to many people, emblematic of a compound failure contributed to by many entities. One of these breakdowns, often cited but not necessarily seen as pre-eminent, is the failure of placemaking in the South Side.

In 2009, I led a delegation of community leaders from Northern Ireland to Chicago. As part of our learning tour, we met with the mayor; we visited the city's LEED-certified offices, which were heralded as making Chicago a leader in sustainability; and we went to the South Side. We toured some of the housing developments and met with some of the agencies and nonprofits working with residents there. The developments were bleak, concrete canyons devoid of beauty and humanity, but the people we met with were committed, caring, and doing their very best. Coming away from those meetings, our visitors from Northern Ireland were absolutely shocked by the conditions they had witnessed. "How can this be possible in America?" was the general sentiment.

How can this be possible in America? How can we allow greatness and hopelessness to exist in such close proximity? The answer is, of course, far more complex than any one book can grasp—I won't even attempt it here. The point is, I now think about Chicago in the context of the "good part of town." If there is nothing nice, redeeming, or even smile-worthy in your neighborhood, then the real negatives of crime and poverty become much, much more possible.

Chicago artist and social entrepreneur Theaster Gates has lived this premise for the past decade. In 2008 he started with a single derelict house in his South Side neighborhood of Grand Crossing. Gates refurbished the house into a multifunction space for art, performances, dinner parties, and community meetings. This became a "hub" and something that the neighborhood could be proud of. Gates noted that people who would never think of visiting the South Side were coming into the neighborhood and leaving with a different perception of what was possible there.[clxii] In the decade since, his Dorchester Projects have spread across the South Side, creating more hubs of activity and beauty, and the ideas have been transplanted and replicated in other cities, including Detroit and my hometown of Akron, Ohio.

Most of us have heard of the so-called "broken windows theory," which posits that small negatives (such as broken windows) lead to more pernicious ones (violent crime). On the South Side of Chicago and other places, we are talking about the broken windows of our souls, which allow blight into our communities when there is not even the smallest bit of hope, beauty or joy. The emotional infrastructure of these South Side neighborhoods had failed, and the standard toolbox of revitalization was not working or was not working fast enough for residents like Gates. When the emotional infrastructure fails, most believe that until you dramatically reduce crime, tear down blighted buildings and clean up the neighborhoods, nothing else is possible. Yes, we should do all of that, but we also need to give people something to believe

Peter Kageyama

in. By reducing crime and blight, you are taking away (some) of the fear. But you have to also pour some love and hope into that place, otherwise it is empty. Though we cannot say definitively that a good park, a mural or a well-designed streetscape will prevent crime and social despair, growing evidence from social science and real world examples like the Dorchester Projects are showing that quality placemaking is one of the necessary bulwarks against those evils.

Quality of place has been seen as commercially oriented and something that affluent communities indulge in— a nice perk but not practical city-building work. It seemed that the very ideas of beauty and "good places" were things some deserved while others did not get. We were never so overt as to say that poor neighborhoods did not deserve beautiful places, but rather we couched it in economic terms and priorities: Because there is more crime and social disruption in this neighborhood, we should focus on policing and basic infrastructure. We can't afford flower boxes in that neighborhood when they have so many other needs.

Bill Strickland is the legendary founder of the Manchester Craftsman's Guild and Bidwell Training Center in Pittsburgh, Pennsylvania. He has been asking why poor people don't deserve flowers, too, as he barnstorms across the country, spreading the gospel of the amazing work his

190

organization does in Pittsburgh. Strickland's afterschool programs and training center are prime examples of the effect of quality places on people and neighborhoods. He talks about treating welfare moms and poor students as worthy of respect, and worthy of beauty and art. The Guild and Bidwell Training Center is famous for having fresh flowers and lots of art on site—and the effect is astounding. Kids from the poorest neighborhoods go through the program and get into college. Former dropouts get training and skills that give them access to good paying jobs. Gang violence and crime stop at the center's doors. Because of this simple idea: Good places make for good people.

Good places—places that are not just functional and safe but have some other human element that we respond to with joy—can play a huge part in the solutions to some of our biggest, most intractable, and complex problems. Good places don't cost lots of money, per se, but building them requires a different sensibility to more than just utility and cost. Such places bring in other things like beauty, art, fun, surprise, and delight— sometimes even unintentionally—into the offering that raises the bar for that place and creates something greater than the sum of its parts. Creative placemaking is often seen as larger and more complex, but it might also be as small as adding a little color to a corner store where people feel comfortable sitting and chatting with each other. It might be creating that pocket park where kids play, or adding some lighting to the existing community center that beckons folks to come inside. We need to see the value of our place-making efforts not just in the economic development, travel and tourism, and talent attraction and retention categories, but also in terms of crime reduction, social justice, environmental sustainability, and overall human health. Every place can and must have something that is good about it. Once we realize that good places are integral to beginning to solve these wicked problems, we might find new value in them, new sources of investment, and a whole new coterie of allies in the effort to make our cities into places that we love.

The Rent Is Too Damn High

In 2005, New York City resident Jimmy McMillan ran for mayor of the metropolis. He didn't win. He ran again in 2009—didn't win. In 2010, he ran for both governor and U.S. senator, and though he again did not win, he amassed over 40,000 votes in the governor's race. McMillan became an online sensation for the simple and highly memorable position of his candidacy: "The rent is too damn high." McMillan channeled a sentiment that resonated not only in New York City, but in many urban areas that had seen an influx of growth and development in recent decades. As people, money, and investment have flowed back into cities, there have been corresponding rises in housing demand, prices, and consumerism. Gentrification is the technical word, but McMillan summed it up by simply and memorably declaring that the rent is too damn high.

Gentrification. The very word raises hackles and invokes images of colonialism, racism, segregation, and classism. Talk about negative emotions! The term was coined in the 1960s by British sociologist Ruth Glass to describe the changes to working class London neighborhoods that occurred as wealthier folks moved in and macro-economic forces pressured working class families to move out. In pure, unemotional terms, gentrification is "the spatial expression of the same large economic forces that have brought us the demise of a blue-collar middle class, the growing advantages of education, and greater inequality."[clxiii] Richard Florida succinctly declared gentrification to be "the location choices of advantaged groups."[clxiv] A bunch of yuppies or hipsters decide your neighborhood is cool and start moving in, driving up rent and housing prices. Soon you find it harder to get a seat at your favorite local restaurant. This is the most benign characterization of gentrification. It can also mean the complete reshaping of historic neighborhoods and the corresponding loss of neighborhood identity. It can even mean the loss of an entire city.

Venice, Italy, is an architectural, historic, and cultural marvel. It is a place that must be seen to be believed. Venice's population plummeted to a new low of 55,000 inhabitants in 2018—down from 164,000 in 1931—as locals fled high rents or found themselves being evicted to make way for tourist accommodations and Airbnb flats. According to the watchdog group Inside Airbnb, more than 6,000 homes or apartments in Venice are dedicated to short term rentals.[clxv]

Venice is an extreme case. Most cities are not dealing with 20 million tourists every year, many arriving on massive cruise ships that dump hundreds of people at a time into the grand old city. Local protesters have even attempted to block these huge ships as they enter the city's waterways.[clxvi] No doubt inflaming the contention is the locals' knowledge that their beloved city is slowly sinking. Scientists estimate that Venice, as we know it, will dip below the waves in 2100[clxvii] if climate change continues on its current course. Regardless of that particular prediction, Venetians know that their city is tenuous and highly susceptible to a natural, or even man-made, disaster. This "Sword of Damocles," perpetually hanging over their heads would no doubt worry even the most optimistic and upbeat of citizens. Sometimes our fears of change overblown. Nearly every community has NIMBY-minded residents who oppose change of any kind. The fears of these diehard downers are usually overblown. But sometimes, in a truly imperiled place like Venice, fears of change and loss of city identity reflect frighteningly real possibilities.

Reykjavik, Iceland, offers a similarly extreme example. In 2008, Iceland underwent a major financial crisis when all three of its major private banks failed, leaving the country in dire financial straits. One of the pillars of its recovery has been the travel and tourism industry. In 2010, Iceland welcomed approximately 500,000 tourists. By 2017, that number exceeded 2 million, with over 25% of visitors coming from the United States.[clxviii] Keep in mind that the entire national population of Iceland is only 353,000 people! At first, this influx was an incredible boon to the country's ailing economy, but as time went by, and more and more people arrived on Iceland's shores, the negative impact of so many tourists began to emerge. Infrastructure gets more wear and tear, transportation systems designed for a smaller population are taxed, the environment is degraded, hotel rooms become scarce, restaurants become harder to get into, and everything becomes more expensive. Locals feel the pinch, then many want to cash in on the tourist trade by converting their spare room or apartment into a short-term rental. This takes actual housing out of the long-term market, driving up housing prices for locals. We will examine this cycle later, but suffice to say that too much of a good thing, like tourists, can lead to some very negative impacts. Recently, Iceland's minister of tourism even called for limits on tourism—a rare message from a tourism official!clxix Iceland needs to find a new balance as a destination for visitors or they risk becoming what Venice has become—a tourist Disneyland where locals play roles like actors on a stage for the entertainment of the audience.

Anti-Gentrification

In February 2014, filmmaker Spike Lee was asked about the changes happening in his beloved Brooklyn. Lee embarked on an epic rant about gentrification that was, of course, captured on social media.clxx He railed against what he described as the "Christopher Columbus syndrome" that newcomers to Brooklyn brought with them. These predominantly white newcomers had "discovered" these neighborhoods even though people of color had been making their lives there for decades. These newcomers, he said, did not respect the local culture and identity, and acted like it needed to change with the arrival of their largely moneyed interests. He talked about a "code" that people should have, to not act like colonizers or worse, saviors of a neighborhood, and he noted with sadness that it was often not until white families moved into the district that local schools improved. All of which is true—however, we are all creatures of self-interest, and it is hard for people to have this kind of self-awareness and understanding. These upwardly mobile families are also accustomed to getting things their way, even without asking for changes. Their economic preferences and tastes become the standard and the expected position. Our city leaders, the developers, and the residents of changing neighborhoods themselves all play a role in gentrification, and few of these stakeholders are effectively planning for the emotional fallout that gentrification precipitates. We are not addressing the fundamental emotional concerns that people feel—anger, mistrust, and the resentments that come with a neighborhood that is changing around us and becoming something alien.

A recent and disturbing trend has been the emergence of confrontational, some would even say "militant," anti-gentrification organizations. These groups organize protests, marches and employ disruptive, sometimes even criminal, tactics to let certain people and organizations know that they are not welcome in a particular community. They have described gentrification as "a vicious, protracted attack on poor and working-class people"[clxxi] and have openly said that the only tactic perpetrators of gentrification respond to is fear. Said one group organizer, "I've found that the only thing that works to stop gentrifiers is intimidation. The only thing that works is fear—the fear of harm."[clxxii]

Groups have organized across the country in cities such as Los Angeles, New York, Chicago, Austin, and Philadelphia. One Philadelphia developer in the Point Breeze neighborhood believes that his residential project was intentionally burned down as part of anti-gentrification efforts.[clxxiii] In South Kensington, another gentrifying neighborhood in Philadelphia, vandals spray painted and damaged new homes and expensive cars.[clxxiv] Developers and new properties, along with new restaurants and coffee shops, are predictable targets, but others are not what you might expect. These targets include art galleries and organizations using art and creative industries to enliven their neighborhoods. There is even a term for this: *artwashing*.

"Artwashing is the use of art and artistic labor to perpetuate and enable gentrification,"[clxxv] says Angel Luna, a resident of the East Los Angeles neighborhood Boyle Heights and a member of the Boyle Heights Alliance Against Artwashing and Displacement (BHAAAD). The arrival of a mural, a local art gallery, or even an arts organization that promotes local artists can be seen as an act of, or prelude to, gentrification.

Boyle Heights, in East Los Angeles, is over 90% Latino and has been one of the epicenters of the aggressive anti-gentrification movement. Two organizations, BHAAAD and Defend Boyle Heights, have arisen in the past few years as the neighborhood began to attract new investment, new businesses, and new residents. In 2017, a local arts organization announced it was closing after a year of dealing with protestors, threats, and lots of unpleasantness at their events. The Defend Boyle Heights group declared victory on social media.

These groups have become *de facto* judges and juries to determine what groups and even what people can come into the neighborhood. There is a tragic irony in the fact that, a generation or so ago, there were militant white groups using similar tactics to keep out families and businesses of color from their neighborhoods. It also seems perverse that these sometimes target artists, who are typically among the more vulnerable members of a community. Many have pointed out that poorer neighborhoods have well established artists and creative industries, and such tactics are diminishing very real opportunities for locally based creators. Recalling the fundamental notion of fairness, if people perceive that they are not going to get at least a portion of some benefit coming to their community—a bite of the proverbial wildebeest—they can turn upon each other, often at the expense of their weaker brethren.

Not all residents in the neighborhood agree with the aggressive approach to anti-gentrification. Steve Almazan, a teacher in Boyle Heights, argued that "the neighborhood shouldn't say, 'Get out—this place is mine.' You want to find a balance. We want investment from the city here." With that investment comes benefits: better schools, safer streets, lighting, streetscaping, parks, transportation nodes. To take the benefits and then tell people and businesses who can and cannot come into the neighborhood is fundamentally flawed. On the other hand, not recognizing how those very investments may be triggers for complex negative economic, social, and cultural externalities is equally flawed.

Gente-fication

Boyle Heights resident and local bar owner Guillermo Uribe is credited with coining the term *gente*-fication. In 2006, he opened a *pocho* bar called Eastside Luv. "Pocho," the word Uribe uses to describe the bar, translates roughly as "Americanized Mexican."[clxxvi] A year later, he began to see changes in Boyle Heights as more Latinos returned to the neighborhood, particularly college-educated Latinos. These people, or *gente* in Spanish, were helping to revitalize the neighborhood. So instead of gentrification from outsiders, Uribe began to sense a certain *gente*-fication—development and investment from Latinos in a predominantly Latino neighborhood. "Gentefication occurs when upwardly mobile, college-educated Latinos return to their old neighborhood and invest their time, money, and interests in [that neighborhood]," says Almazan. "I'll come out and say I consider myself a gentefier."[clxxvii]

"If gentrification is happening, it might as well be from people who care about the existing culture…because they are more likely to preserve its integrity,"[clxxviii] said Uribe.

Uribe's distinction seems totally reasonable to me and might even point to a strategy for mitigating gentrification. Yet his FUBU ("for us by us") mindset is not shared by all in the neighborhood. The Defend Boyle Heights organization noted that even Latino-owned businesses may be inadvertently promoting gentrification when their actions attract outsiders. Alleged offenses include such seemingly innocent events as the annual Day of the Dead celebration. One local business was taken to task because its successful event brought in outside visitors and tourists to the neighborhood.

Barney Santos is the founder of Gentefy, an incubator for Latino-owned businesses in underserved neighborhoods of

Los Angeles. He argues that "we need to bring new businesses into the neighborhood, but at the same time invest in the legacy businesses that are already here."[clxxix] Sadly, there seems to be almost a purity test to see how authentic, how local, even how Latino, someone actually is. Recall the arts organization in Boyle Heights that became the locus of the anger. Some see artists and arts organizations as being the advance guard of the gentrification process. However there is abundant evidence that artists and arts organizations do not cause gentrification. A 2016 study[clxxx] that looked at multiple zip codes across three continents found that arts organizations and businesses tended to cluster in already established (i.e., already gentrified) areas or in areas that had "no potential to gentrify."[clxxxi] Interestingly the study noted that "gentrifying neighborhoods actually had the smallest concentration of, and slowest growth in, arts establishments."[clxxxii] Arts organizations and businesses tend to locate where their likely customers are – in well-established neighborhoods or somewhere they can find really cheap rents. Neighborhoods that are in the process of changing and potentially becoming gentrified are the least likely locations for such businesses.

Even if most arts establishments are located in well established, middle and upper middle-class neighborhoods, this statistical fact doesn't account for the very real emotional impact that the emergence of newcomers, including arts and cultural establishments, have on a neighborhood. There is a noticeable impact when something new and different arrives in our ecosystem. We *notice* something that changes the community equilibrium. So, while in statistical terms a single gallery opening in a neighborhood might not mean much, it can have immense emotional and psychological impact for that place. A single intervention can be highly disruptive to our sense of place, for good or ill. Moreover, one disruption sends a signal to other potential disrupters that change is happening. In that sense, I do not believe it is the arts groups and artists that spur gentrification but rather the secondary cohort that observes and orbits these artists. Clearly there are restaurateurs, retailers and developers that pay attention to where and when certain sentinel entities alight.

In zoological circles, a sentinel species is one that marks the presence of something dangerous to us as human beings. The canary in the coal mine is the classic example of the sentinel species. The canary is more susceptible to noxious gases in the mine, and its distress warns miners that a problem is developing. In this analogy, artists are a sentinel species for gentrification. The image reminds me of writer Kurt Vonnegut's famous characterization of the role of the artist:

I sometimes wondered what the use of any of the arts was. The best thing I could come up with was what I call the canary in the coal mine theory of the arts. This theory says that artists are useful to society because they are so sensitive. They are super-sensitive. They keel over like canaries in poison coal mines long before more robust types realize that there is any danger whatsoever.[clxxxiii]

In this sense, even a single art gallery might put us on high alert, but to blame them for macro social and economic changes in a neighborhood is misguided. Activists will point to the fact that these newcomers are complicit in gentrification because they make a choice to come into a neighborhood—therefore, they become targets of backlash. This outlook is lazy and short sighted. Yes, you can blame the newcomers, scare away the gallery owner, and force the closure of the coffee shop. But these tactics do not, even remotely, address the underlying problems precipitating gentrification.

Anti-gentrification groups call for better jobs, higher wages, and more opportunities; closing a neighborhood business does nothing to address those fundamental needs. Though some may call this is a victory and believe that it will achieve their goals, such action at best postpones the process. Perhaps the individual gallery owner or developer is driven off. But there is always going to be another developer, businessperson or entrepreneur who will see the opportunity and take the risk.

When outsiders become interested in a neighborhood, this interest may present both a crisis and an opportunity to residents. Rather than taking to the streets, how could you take advantage of the attention and interest people are paying to your neighborhood? Could you use the implied threat of protest to secure better opportunities for your community? Community Benefits Agreements between developers and neighborhoods are becoming more common. These agreements allow neighborhoods to bargain collectively with developers to include more affordable housing, more jobs in associated new establishments, and better wages for locals who are hired. Addressing many other community needs and desires is also possible. Ultimately, community groups could become the managers and administrators of these relationships and perhaps even provide a seal of approval of some sort to developers. Could Defend Boyle Heights become an economic watchdog that calls bullshit on businesses that come into a neighborhood, then don't hire locals or give back to their community?

Politically, you can force your local city council to address substantive policy changes such as mandatory inclusionary zoning, "no chain" zones or community design standards. No politician wants to look bad, and activist groups have shown an ability to organize, get loud and draw attention to issues. While they may not have PAC-level money, these kinds of people and groups can sway elections because they get people motivated.

How about simply throwing your hat in the ring and running for office? The past few years have witnessed impressive wins by anti-establishment, untraditional candidates on both sides of the political spectrum. From a transgendered state representative in Virginia (Danica Roem) to a 28-year old democratic socialist in New York (Alexandria Ocasio-Cortez), the political doors are opening to new possibilities—and that seems to scare the hell out of traditional power on both sides of the political spectrum. Taking to the streets may be a pathway to a small—and, I believe, temporary—victory, but it is in the ability to organize and inspire people to action that movements can effectuate real and lasting change.

It is noteworthy that the main outbursts of militant anti-gentrification are coming from young people of color. Yes, they are angry, but I believe they are scared, more than anything else. Millennials' lives are being shaped by a bleak economic future. On the whole, they have incurred 300% more debt than their parents.[clxxxiv] For them, employment is far more short term and gig-based than career oriented. Health care costs are rising, and their very health is declining. This generation of Americans, for the first time in over 25 years, has a lower life expectancy than their parents.[clxxxv] And among millennials of color, these conditions are exacerbated. Their generation has seen the wage gap between the 1% and the 99% grow to unprecedented levels. The world looks increasingly unfair from their vantage point, so it is little wonder that they are reacting with fear and anger to a situation they did not create.

Clearly, Angel Luna and those who are taking to the streets in defense of their neighborhoods love their communities. I applaud that—and I want to help them continue to live in and love those communities. While there appear to be some successes in Boyle Heights and other communities where aggressive anti-gentrification groups have formed, I see little long-term hope for them. Either economic opportunity moves on to another area, or another entity arises that is willing to take the heat and move forward. While I have no doubt that the founders of anti-gentrification organizations are highly motivated, at some point, their time will be divided by other commitments and opportunities. Patient money—and there is always patient money—will eventually find a foothold.

What Can We Do?

While such militant groups can seem unwilling to

compromise, they do raise some very important issues. Affordable housing is at the crux of fears about gentrification. While measures such as inclusionary zoning seek to ensure a baseline of affordable housing, even that approach is problematic for poorer neighborhoods. "Affordable" is based on a formula for determining average household incomes in a region. Angel Luna noted that for Los Angeles County the median income is $55,000, yet for Boyle Heights (a neighborhood in L.A. County) the median is $34,000.[clxxxvi] Average household income is a function of census data, and it has been well established that minority populations, especially communities of immigrants (both legal and illegal), are notoriously difficult to model and account for correctly. This further skews the numbers, as it most likely does not account for an impoverished shadow class living outside the counted realm.

Inclusionary zoning is a prime example of how cities have struggled when seeking to intervene in the market forces that drive gentrification. During the late 20th century, inclusionary zoning was developed as an attempt to reverse the consequences of racially motivated red-lining of districts, outdated zoning regulations, along with market and other macro forces that shaped the suburban sprawl following World War II. By requiring a certain percentage of new development to be allocated as affordable housing, this zoning practice hoped to created urban developments that were not economically segregated and allow long time residents the opportunity to stay in their community, even as the neighborhood was changing and improving around them. Results have been mixed and while inclusionary zoning remains a tool in the urban toolkit, it is only part of an increasingly complex environment. A hot button area where this confluence of zoning, technology, entrepreneurship, and property rights have collided is the short-term rental industry ignited by Airbnb.

The Airbnb Dilemma

Airbnb, the widely used homestay and house rental application, was born in San Francisco in 2008. The company's founders had been running a small business providing overnight accommodations to convention attendees—mostly younger, tech-centric visitors from across the country. They set up air mattresses in a loft and charged a few bucks for an overnight stay. They soon realized the real need and potential market for short-term rentals. By 2011, one million room nights had been booked through the platform.[clxxxvii] By 2012, five million nights had been booked;[clxxxviii] in 2017 alone, over 100 million nights were booked worldwide.[clxxxix] Airbnb has had phenomenal impact on the sharing economy. However, with its exponential growth has come very real challenges for cities as they now struggle to incorporate and regulate the emergent short-term rental market.

Initially, the hotel and hospitality industry called for regulation of Airbnb and the other major player, VRBO, which it perceived as direct competitors. As such platforms expanded, municipalities joined in the choir calling for regulation and taxes, especially as the impacts of short-term rentals on neighborhoods and cities started to become apparent. One study from McGill University's School of Urban Planning, titled "The High Cost of Short-Term Rentals in New York City," indicated that between 2014 and 2017 rents in NYC had risen 1.4% in response to short-term rental demand, equivalent to an average increase of $340 per month.[cxc] This study and others like it were rebutted by Airbnb based on questions of their methodology and other technical factors.[cxci] What is not really in dispute is the sheer number of rental properties that were eliminated from the market by conversion to short term rentals. It is estimated that between 7,000 and 13,500 rental properties in New York were removed from the (long-term rental) market,[cxcii] thus putting greater pressure upon New York City's already tight market for rental homes. Methodology aside, it seems obvious that if you remove long-term rentals from a neighborhood, supply becomes scarcer and those rentals that remain fetch premium rates.

Some cities have responded with outright prohibitions on short-term rentals, citing zoning ordinances that prohibit businesses in residential areas. Others, such as Seattle, have moved to classify short-term rentals into categories and tax them approximately $8 to $14 per night, based on whether the rental space is a separate apartment or a shared space.[cxciii] Boston moved to prevent a "power host" situation by prohibiting investor properties where owners do not live on or near the rental property.[cxciv]

A significant part of the challenge lies in the undocumented or illegal registration of short-term rentals. Reykjavik, Iceland, has been rocked by the explosive growth of tourism, coupled with rampant proliferation of short-term rentals. The City of Reykjavik estimates that housing prices rose by 5-9% between 2015 and 2017.[cxcv] The city requires all short-term rental owners to register as a business if they rent more than 90 nights per year, but officials believe that more than 60% of owners do not register.[cxcvi] They estimate that over 1,400 properties are incorrectly listed, thus depriving the city of an estimated 1 billion krona, or nearly $10 million U.S. dollars, in annual taxes.

Airbnb and VRBO are forcing city and state

governments to respond. Governments are trying to use existing regulatory frameworks, but technology will always move faster than regulators, so it is not a surprise that the short-term rental industry has proved a particular challenge. Another reason is that the business of short-term rentals touches on fundamental notions in our society of personal freedom and property rights.

I consider myself a fan of Airbnb, as the company's basic belief in experiencing local neighborhoods and meeting local people is congruent with my passion for fostering greater emotional engagement with places. It also seems to me to be a good thing when participating in the short-term rental economy allows local homeowners to monetize their spare room or garage apartment, thus adding to economic opportunities in specific communities. The problematic side-effects of Airbnb-type businesses do not stem from mom-and-pop rentals offered by on-site homeowners; the problem arises from larger-scale purchases of properties and mass rentals that are *de facto* hotels. A 2016 study showed that in major metro areas, 12% of total renters accounted for 45% of all rentals, meaning that a small group of "power hosts" controlled large numbers of units and a sizeable proportion of all listings. The rampant proliferation of such rentals, which are really larger-scale hospitality ventures masquerading as small businesses, is putting stress on neighborhoods unlike anything previously seen. While some locals may be profiting from the platform, many absentee owners renting out units have little or no connection to a given neighborhood.

As a result, resentments are growing. A personal friend of mine related a story about a trip he and his family made to San Diego. Via Airbnb, they had rented a home for a long weekend in an upscale neighborhood in the city. Upon arrival, they discovered that the house had been vandalized, but perhaps not in the way you might imagine. Cable boxes had been thrown into the swimming pool, furniture overturned but not damaged, cabinets emptied but not destroyed. It seemed that the vandals, perhaps distraught neighbors, wanted to send a message to the owner and Airbnb users that short-term rentals were not welcome in the neighborhood. My friend reported that his family opted to check into a hotel, rather than stay on the property.

One online commenter brilliantly and succinctly analyzed the Airbnb model when they said, "Airbnb has always struck me as a good *small* idea but a terrible *big* idea. That's because it doesn't understand housing and isn't designed to."cxcvii The same commenter noted that they felt like a performer for the many Airbnb guests that rotate through their own New York City neighborhood. Housing is more than an economic good, of course. If we reduce housing and neighborhoods to commodities, which Airbnb and VRBO are designed to do, it is easy to suggest throwing open the gates and letting homeowners freely trade and operate as they see fit. But housing exists in the context of the social and cultural space of a neighborhood, and that neighborhood adds significant value to the property. Four walls, a bed and a toilet can be found in lots of places, but those same four walls in Greenwich Village, Dupont Circle or downtown Reykjavik are very different places.

Where does one person's property rights (e.g., the right to rent their property) begin to impinge, with negative effect, on another person's property rights? This is an economic and legal question, to be sure, but one with emotional dimensions and consequences.

How is this different from Uber?

In my previous book, *Love Where You Live*, I wrote about the ride-sharing service Uber. I made the point then that millennials and their attitudes about cars and mobility were forcing cities into a somewhat reluctant acceptance of ride-sharing services. Just a few years ago, Uber and its leading rival, Lyft, faced many regulatory challenges and conflicts with traditional taxi and limo services. Some jurisdictions attempted to make the ride-sharing services comply with existing taxi regulations. In Tampa, Florida, legislators proposed instituting a $7 minimum per ride and a minimum 7-minute wait before the car arrives.[cxcviii] (That was certainly one of the most arbitrary and absurd responses to change I have seen.) The move seemed to imply that the Tampa lawmakers were desperate to slow down a service too good for traditional competitors to challenge without artificial limitations.

Today, nearly every city and state has come to equilibrium with ride-sharing services, and we accept them as part of the standard offerings in cities both big and small. How is this aspect of the sharing economy different from Airbnb and VRBO?

Ride-sharing services emerged in large part for a very basic reason: almost universally, taxi services suck. Most of us have had the experience of calling a dispatcher, requesting a cab and waiting, waiting and waiting. You might call back, and they'd say the cab will be right there. Uncertainty reigns as your frustration grows. Into this gap stepped the ride-sharing platforms and nearly everyone, except cab and limo companies, rejoiced. Ride-sharing companies disintermediated and dislocated the transportation industry. Taxi medallions in New York City, once worth upwards of $1 million each, now trade at around $200,000.[cxcix] That is a very real decline in the value of medallions, and I am sympathetic to drivers whose personal finances were affected. However, this cycle of creative destruction has been repeated over and over in every industry. Technology and culture shifts, a new market emerges, and another gets left behind. The horse and buggy industry, the downtown department store (see Chapter Four) and videocassette rental are now footnotes in business history. We accept this and move on.

Why does Airbnb feel different? Because short-term rental services are not disintermediating businesses and industry. In fact, the hotel industry has continued to grow over the lifetime of Airbnb,[cc] and industry experts tout the next twenty-five years as a "golden age" for hoteliers.[cci] Even traditional bed-and-breakfasts remain strong, according to Association of Independent Hospitality Professionals.[ccii] If Airbnb is not disintermediating the hotel and hospitality industry, who is it affecting? It appears to be all of us, the people who live in neighborhoods, people who may or may not own property but call a place our home. Defend Boyle Heights may have targeted art galleries and hipster coffee shops, but it is far more likely for the less visible impact of well-meaning locals renting out rooms or apartments to spur the gentrification process locals fear. Airbnb turns us into competitors in a game of which most of us don't fully understand the stakes. Those stakes are no less than the heart and soul of our neighborhoods.

The Problem and the Missing Elements of the Solution

Gentrification is seen as a major economic problem and has resulted in a wide range of economic responses. But is it really a problem of such magnitude, and is it actually an economic problem, per se? The short answer to both questions is "yes," but not for the reasons you might think.

A 2001 Brookings Institute report posits that the term gentrification is both "imprecise and politically charged."[cciii] The term is imprecise because technical definitions vary, as people try to define a set of conditions that seem at once obvious yet highly variable. Defining gentrification through calculation requires technical expertise and access to data: comparing average incomes below median to actual housing costs, for instance. However, most people would agree that rapidly rising housing costs, rising to the point that they begin to outstrip the average earning capacity of resident households, is a key condition of gentrification. A rise in housing costs puts pressure on neighborhoods, potentially forcing long-term residents to leave. This is the central pillar of objections to gentrification—the economic dislocation caused by rising costs. If you were to ask most people, they would tell you that it is happening in many parts of their cities and that it is happening constantly. People feel that gentrification is a very real, very common occurrence; in reality, it is not.

A 2016 study by New York University's Furman Center for Real Estate and Urban Policy noted that about 25% of New York City neighborhoods were gentrifying, based on the numbers they studied.[cciv] One in four neighborhoods is not as high as one might imagine, especially given the dynamic urban environment of New York City. But further research shows that the actual numbers of people forced out of their neighborhoods by economic forces is remarkably low.

Dr. Lance Freeman of Columbia University's Urban Planning program has studied this problem for decades and has stated that actual displacement occurs in a surprisingly low percentage of instances; in fact, only 1.3% of the time.[ccv] Other research on renters found that renters in gentrifying neighborhoods faced only a 2.6 percent higher risk of displacement.[ccvi] Freeman found that poor households in non-gentrifying neighborhoods were actually more likely to have to move out than in gentrifying neighborhoods.[ccvii] Newcomers are often better off and can appreciably change the median income of an area but not necessarily drive out long-time residents. In a 2004 study, Freeman "found that a neighborhood's poverty rate could drop from 30 percent to 12 percent in a decade with minimal displacement. That's because gentrification often leads to new construction or to investment in once-vacant properties."[ccviii]

Yet despite this evidence, the perception of gentrification and displacement as a leading and ubiquitous problem of city life is commonplace. I liken it to the fear of shark attacks that followed the release of the movie *Jaws* in 1975. Yes, sharks exist and, yes, hypothetically, you could be attacked, but the probability of being the victim of a shark attack is very, very small. (Of course, such logic held no sway with my teenage self as I nervously eyeballed the Atlantic Ocean on a summer trip with my father to the beaches of North Carolina). This is the crux of the challenge for us as city makers: gentrification is a significant problem because it is perceived as a significant problem. It is perceived as a significant problem because it is an economic situation with immense and complex emotional dimensions. It is that emotional component that is not given enough credence and attention. As a result, our current efforts to address gentrification are failing to connect with the challenges, fears, and potential opportunities for our communities.

Even when cities seemingly do everything right—rewriting outdated ordinances, hiring experts on urban policy, housing or social justice, and including affordable housing measures—they still run headlong into challenges, neighborhood resistance and fear. In 2014, the City of Austin, Texas, as part of its comprehensive planning process, revamped their code and zoning process, launching an updated system called CodeNEXT. The process was described as a "deep clean"[ccix] of their code and was a textbook example of the kinds of changes planners and policy experts recommend. However, in August 2018, the mayor of Austin called upon the city to scrap nearly four years of work and start over.

"We had been hoping for a process that would bring Austin together and result in a code that would help us solve many of our biggest challenges. However, CodeNEXT and the community discussion surrounding it have largely been contentious and marked with misinformation," said Austin Mayor Steve Adler. "It is becoming increasingly apparent that the CodeNEXT process, so divisive and poisoned, will not get us to a better place."[ccx] The city did scrap the project and in the spring of 2019, began to discuss how they would shape the process and try once again to draft the next generation code.[ccxi]

If the best of efforts to address gentrification can fail, it highlights a fundamental gap in our approach to a most vexing problem. We are failing to address the huge emotional component of these issues. We make technical and economic arguments but in doing this we have not taken into full account people's often complex feelings about their neighborhood, the future, and their place in it.

Root Shock

Kay Hymowitz, author and Fellow with the Manhattan Institute for Policy Research, notes in her research of gentrification, "The urge to hold on to familiar landscapes and ways of living is as human as memory itself. Change is happening in many cities so fast and so dramatically that it overwhelms all sense of continuity and violates our urge to believe in the enduring solidity of places and things."[ccxii] When we react to gentrification, what we are reacting to, are not the primarily economic forces, but the cultural and emotional implications of gentrification. Spike Lee's condemnation was not just economic, but about a lack of respect for the culture and history that existed in Brooklyn long before hipsters arrived.

Western democracies, particularly the United States, have a deep and abiding love of market economies. We lionize entrepreneurs and business success stories, hold them up and say that the markets have spoken, and that we should respect and abide by the judgment of markets. However, "free" markets can be cruel and deeply unfair. They favor those with capital, scientific or technological advantages and lots of entrenched power.

What city leaders, developers, activists and community representatives can and should do is attempt to mitigate the negative outcomes associated with gentrification. These outcomes often are not economic. No owner is going to be upset about increasing property values. No resident is going to decry the arrival of a supermarket or better restaurants. The negatives around gentrification are the fear of change and the unknown future it holds. Clearly, fear of economic dislocation is part of this equation. But, as has been noted, the actual numbers of people being forced out of their neighborhoods is much smaller than the perception of dislocation. The fear, however, is very real. A far more likely scenario is less dramatic but just as immediate.

As Hymowitz notes, the rapidity of change can "overwhelm our sense of continuity," which is a fancy way of saying we are afraid we won't like our new neighbors. Think about it—the fundamental fear of gentrification is the loss of our familiar friends and neighbors to an unknown future. It is the loss of social capital that is the most impactful and worries us the most. In plain terms, it is the loss of relationships that worries us far more than economic impacts, but it is the economic side of gentrification that gets most of our attention. Think about the pain of a lost relationship versus the pain of lost money. Money comes and goes, and while none of us want to lose money, we know that the particular fear and angst of financial loss passes relatively quickly. As human beings, what we truly fear is the loss of relationships. Few things are as painful and lasting as the loss of a significant other, a family member or a friend. We feel these loses in ways that money and economics can't rival.

What cities can and should do is invest in programs and projects that increase neighborhood social capital and help to restore and build relationships. If we can bring new and old residents together more quickly, and facilitate social connections between them, we can remove the largest and most pernicious externalities of gentrification.

In the Philadelphia neighborhood of Germantown, some local businesses have attempted to address this problem in an intentional manner. Germantown is a traditionally African American neighborhood (over 80%) but has recently started to see the arrival of new, mostly white, and wealthier faces. Philadelphia is one of the most racially segregated cities in the U.S..[ccxiii] but Germantown is one of its most ethnically diverse neighborhoods. It is that very diversity that has attracted many of the neighborhood's newest residents. These newcomers and long-term residents need opportunities to get to know each other, and that is exactly what happens at Uncle

Bobbie's Coffee and Books, and the Germantown Espresso Bar.

Uncle Bobbie's Coffee & Books is a labor of love for Temple University professor Marc Lamont Hill. Hill, a prominent African American author and political commentator, wanted to give something back to his neighborhood. In 2017, he opened Uncle Bobbie's (named after his real-life uncle) because he believed in "the power of community."[ccxiv] He believed that urban coffee shop culture in general wasn't really friendly to black or brown people. Unfortunately, his suspicion was confirmed on April 12, 2018, when two black men in Philadelphia were arrested for sitting and waiting for a friend in a downtown Starbucks. Hill's concept for Uncle Bobbie's was an inclusive space intentionally designed to bring in the local community. He talked about "Shoppe Black," the national movement to encourage African Americans to shop at African American-owned businesses, as an influence. Uncle Bobbie's serves coffee and sells books, but what it really provides is a place where all people feel comfortable. It's an example of how to bring an entire community together without forcing or cajoling people to do the right thing.

Nearby, the Germantown Espresso Bar could easily be seen as an archetypal gentrifying business. The coffee shop is owned by Miles Butler and Jeff Podlogar, two young white men; Podlogar even sports the trademark hipster beard. However, Butler is from Germantown. Their space is part coffee shop, part meeting space, part performance space with a very popular open mic night that appeals to all manner of participants. Sensitivity to the local community appears to be a key ingredient in their success.

"While we're very aware that we are two white men, we are for and by the community," Butler says. "Having grown up here, I'm sensitive to the racial and class divisions in the community."[ccxv]

Both projects are examples of *gentefication*, if you will. While the term has its roots in the Latino community, I believe it needs to be expanded and adopted by neighborhoods everywhere as a framework for their own local love efforts. Pioneering local businesses and residents have realized, astutely, that communities need more than jobs and infrastructure. They need places where people come together, places where they can interact with each other organically, without a forced notion of community. In doing so, people who mix and mingle demystify and destigmatize each other. In this vein, city leaders should look to invest more in such incubators of social capital as they seek to address the effects of gentrification.

Investments such as new community centers and public commons including plazas, parks, playgrounds, and dog parks are good examples. Others include programs such as block parties, beautification projects that engage members of local communities in leadership roles, public art that reflects neighborhood identities, and "buy local" campaigns that preserve and protect the retail history of places from national brands that do nothing to bolster a sense of local identity. In Fort Collins, Colorado, matching facade grants of up to $5,000 are provided to established businesses to update their storefronts to remain in place and stay competitive with newcomers. Small investments, targeted towards mitigating the negatives of gentrification and economic disparity, can be hugely impactful, particularly on the emotional side of the problem.

Trying to fight the macroeconomic forces entwined with gentrification would be a gargantuan and philosophically difficult battle. Think about this question: How much control do we want to cede to government forces, even for the most well-meaning reasons, to control market economic forces? Many conservatives have a deep, philosophical distrust of government, and even moderates and progressives who believe that government (if done well) can be a force for good recognize that regulation can have unintended consequences.

Where we need more activity is in the small, hyper-local opportunities to help connect new and old residents, and to help those displaced by macro-scale forces find new friends and neighbors and establish meaningful relationships. Small-scale efforts can easily be recalibrated as conditions change or results emerge that we did not plan, necessitating course correction. It is in these small solutions that we may begin to solve the big, intractable, and emotionally complex problems. I'm not suggesting that we give up on the systems-scale planning and updating of our codes and regulatory frameworks. What is becoming increasingly clear, though, is that traditional approaches, however well-intentioned, inclusive and smart, are increasingly facing challenges from highly emotional citizenry in contested neighborhoods. To try to quell such unease with more meetings, more information, and more "outreach" without considering the emotional component of the conflict will continue to fall flat and result in further distance between city officials and their residents.

Peter Kageyama

CHAPTER 8 – THE POWER OF RECURSION

The 1984 movie *The Karate Kid* is, for my money, one of the finest martial arts movies ever made. Not because of the fights or the choreography—Bruce Lee is the indisputable champion in that category—but because of the spirit and message of the film. Mr. Miyagi, portrayed by actor Pat Morita, is a teacher any of us would be lucky to have. One iconic scene in the film holds a powerful lesson for everyone.

Daniel, played by Ralph Macchio, is tasked with washing and waxing Mr. Miyagi's cars. He is shown very specifically how to do this by using a pair of gestures that Mr. Miyagi describes with famous brevity: "Wax on. Wax off." Daniel spends the next several hours doing just that. The next day, he is shown how to sand the deck and paint the fence of the house—again, with very specific instructions. Daniel follows the prescribed steps, but he becomes increasingly frustrated that his teacher is not teaching him karate. Only later, when Mr. Miyagi explains to Daniel that he has actually learned fundamental movements in karate through the process of doing various chores, does Daniel appreciate the lesson.

What Mr. Miyagi did was teach Daniel some very small and simple things, over and over, until those small moves actually helped Daniel solve a bigger problem. In the film, Daniel's big problem is how to avoid being destroyed in the upcoming karate tournament by a much more skilled fighter. Miyagi knows that he cannot solve the big problem directly—you cannot train a true black belt in six weeks, but you can address smaller, more immediate problems that build towards a larger solution.

In the realm of computer science, this process has a name—recursion. Recursion is one of the central ideas and principals of computer programming. Here's a technical definition:

A computer programming technique involving the use of a procedure, subroutine, function, or algorithm that calls itself one or more times until a specified condition is met, at which time the rest of each repetition is processed from the last one called to the first.[ccxvi]

In practice, recursion was a way for computer programmers to repeatedly call up a subroutine to solve a small recurring problem. They used this as an efficient way to write code that wasn't bulky and could be run faster, particularly on hardware platforms with limited processing power. Thus, programmers would use a small solution to help solve a larger, more intractable problem. Wax on, wax off.

I actually have a bit of technology background. In the mid-1990s, I co-founded a web development shop with my best friend and former band mate, Ken Walker. As Ken said, I knew just enough about the technology to be dangerous. (I hope that's still the case)! Not coming from a computer science background, I missed the early days of punch card programming, Basic, Fortran, Cobol and other now-archaic technology. I didn't learn about recursion until recently. It took a serendipitous meeting to make me realize that the concept had potential implications, beyond computer science, for our communities.

In the spring of 2017, I visited Muncie, Indiana. As part of my visit, my hosts from the city introduced me to community leaders in the Muncie neighborhood called Whitely. It is an historically African-American neighborhood in Muncie and for a long time, it had been among the more economically challenged parts of town. Neighborhood leaders told me that, in the fall of 2015, with the assistance of Ball State professor Peter Ellery and his landscape architecture class, they held a series of community meetings designed to create a plan for the neighborhood. One of their main goals was to attract a supermarket to the area.

Rebecca Parker is one of the board members of the Whitely Community Council, a nonprofit that serves the neighborhood. She explained that a theme emerged from the meetings: residents thought it would be great if the neighborhood had a "look," and their inspiration was a particular affordable housing development in the neighborhood. Opened a few years prior, this affordable housing project was well-designed with a bright, pastel color palette. Parker said the neighborhood liked the aesthetic and decided "we can take that color palette and extend it out and create a sort of visual identity for the neighborhood."

The Council raised around $6000 for paint and supplies, and they christened 2016 as the Whitely Year of Color. They partnered with the City's Parks & Recreation Department along the way. This was critical, because one of the centerpieces of the neighborhood is McColloch Park, the largest park in Muncie. Neighborhood residents wanted to paint and fix up parts of the park, including the playground, benches, and tables. This required the support of Harvey

Wright, the head of the parks department. Wright was an enthusiastic supporter from the outset. Parker said "he was an amazing partner the whole way through. He really loves seeing people taking ownership of their communities and especially their public assets."

In the spring of 2016, residents of Whitely began the process of painting their neighborhood. They worked with a local teen organization, Teenwork, to help prepare the park for painting before a dedicated Paint the Park Day. When Paint the Park Day arrived, more than 140 volunteers came out to be part of the process. Said Parker: "It felt kind of magical. I mean, all these people were coming together to make their neighborhood park safer and cleaner and more beautiful. So, we didn't just paint that day. We also did cleanup in the park. So we picked up trash. We also fixed the medians, because we had several medians that needed to be weeded and replanted and mulched, so we did that as well. So, I mean, lots of things got done in the park that made a huge visual difference in one day."

People painted mailboxes, doors, steps, and sign posts. They went into McColloch Park and painted the playground, the equipment, the benches and tables. They even got permission to paint the fire hydrants.

Peter Kageyama

Without a doubt, this was a wonderful community project. It certainly is the kind of "love note" I encourage—the relatively small, inexpensive change that has an outsized impact on the community. But in addition to bringing people together, creating social capital and beautifying the neighborhood, some other amazing things started to happen in Whitely. The parks department director noted that the area got safer. Because of the bright colors, people started looking at the park more, which resulted in more attention being paid to what goes on there. Crime, such as drug deals and prostitution, declined. As the park got safer, more people started to use the park, which in turn made it even safer. These positive activities encouraged more people to use the park, thus driving out illegal and unsavory activities in a positive cycle. Today, McColloch Park is a well-used and much loved community asset. Social capital in the neighborhood has gone up, certainly local pride has gone up, and I expect home values have risen as well. All this coming from a coat of paint. The momentum has continued and as of the spring of 2019, the Whitely Community Council had purchased a long vacant building with the plan to renovate it and lure a supermarket or co-op to the neighborhood.

If I challenged your community with the problem of how to reduce crime in your neighborhood and your budget was $6000, you would be hard pressed to come up with a solution. That much money might pay overtime for one officer for part of the year, train one police dog, or install a few new tires on police cruisers that patrol the neighborhood. Crime and public safety is one of those big, intractable, "wicked" problems that defy our best efforts to solve or even manage. Collectively, we spend billions on this problem every year—with a wide range of results. Yet, in the previous example, we see a simple, inexpensive project that seems to break the rules and expectations of what is a public safety initiative. The closest analogy I can come up with is the so-called Broken Window Theory, made famous in New York City under former Mayor Rudy Giuliani. Its motivation was to prevent small, pervasive negative activities and the resulting negative externalities. Petty crimes were harshly punished and broken windows and graffiti were quickly repaired, lest they encourage more of the same. The core notion was that if the streets were clean, people are psychologically less likely to litter or vandalize the environment. Unlike fixing the broken windows, the idea behind the Whitely Year of Color is to increase and incentivize positive reactions to the environment instead of preventing negative behaviors in the community. The reduction in the negative is wonderful side effect of the process.

Planting Flowers

Sullivan County sits amid the Catskill Mountains in

southern New York. Located some 70 miles northwest of New York City, the county was a tourist destination known as the Borscht Belt for much of the 20th century. The area's hotels and resorts, predominantly owned and operated by European Jews, became part of popular culture after World War II, commemorated in films such as *Dirty Dancing*. By the 1970s and 80s, Catskills resorts had entered a decline caused by changing tastes and cheap airfare. New Yorkers who wanted to escape the city during the summer now had unlimited options for spending their travel dollars. As a result, Sullivan County, along with neighboring Ulster and Orange counties, fell into a downturn.

In 2000, a group of Sullivan County residents formed a working group with a simple mission: planting flowers across the region. At first, their idea was met with polite smiles and skepticism. The town administrator for Fallsburg, Steven Vegliante, said he originally thought the idea of planting flowers, when there were so many more serious problems to address, was foolish. I heard this from Vegliante himself as he spoke at the Bethel Woods Performing Arts Center in the heart of Sullivan County. He was there to receive an award for his city, and I was speaking to the group. Vegliante explained that he had been completely wrong about the importance of planting those flowers. That the simple act led to so many positive changes—including, he noted, the incredible performing arts center we then sat in.

America In Bloom (AIB) is a fantastic organization that I have come to know over the years. I first spoke to them as a group in 2013 and have developed an ongoing relationship with the organization ever since. Formed in 2001 and modeled after European organizations that helped to beautify their communities through landscaping, plants, and flowers, AIB helps communities find their inner beauty. They provide the expertise and best practices around urban horticulture, but what they really do is bring together ordinary citizens who care about their neighborhoods and give them the tools and the focus to make something happen. AIB volunteers come together, roll up their sleeves, and get dirty together. They weed, they plant, they paint—and since their founding they have worked with more than 240 cities in 41 states.

AIB has formalized a recursive process. Planting a flower, or a tree, is far more than just that gesture. It is a physical act of making that requires us to roll up our sleeves and get a little dirty. Planting has been a central pillar of our civilization for thousands of years and it connects us in visceral and profound ways to the work, to the land, and to each other. It is an act of renewal. Unlike a mural, the planting of flowers and trees does not require any artistic ability and it involves a living entity. As we have discussed elsewhere in this book, our biophilic need to connect with other living things is powerful, and can be tapped into and shared with the broader community. Though AIB wouldn't characterize their work in this way, they are actually teaching recursion to the cities with whom they work. These cities most likely don't even realize everything they are learning through the process, which they may understand simply as landscaping or beautification (which it is, on one level). If both sides were more cognizant of the underlying significance of the process and sought ways to continue it, they might even be able to focus such energy and enthusiasm toward needs in other directions, and into other, bigger problems.

Wicked Problems

In other domains, we see how small solutions impact bigger problems. In my hometown of St. Petersburg, Florida a "ban the straw" movement is afoot. Not unique to St. Pete, this movement is spreading all over the U.S. and many parts of the world. It frames the issue with striking simplicity: ask restaurants and fast food establishments not to use or automatically provide plastic straws with drinks. Why? Because all those little straws add up to a literal mountain of plastic waste in our environment.

According to EcoCycle, a U.S. based nonprofit recycling group, the U.S. alone uses 500 million plastic straws every day.[ccxvii] Each of those straws has about a 200-year life cycle. *The New York Times* has noted that "plastic straws kill marine life and choke reefs and beaches, never decomposing completely, but instead breaking into bits of microplastics, which eventually enter the food chain."[ccxviii] Yeah, we end up eating those same straws. Companies including Starbucks, Marriott, and Royal Caribbean Cruises have also declared the end of their use of plastic straws.[ccxix] In 2018, the entire country of England announced plans to end the use of plastic straws and plastic swabs.[ccxx] Most of us would not think twice about a straw, but this little change could trigger a significant shift in the global environment and in overall human health.

On December 13, 2018, the city council of St. Petersburg formally voted to ban the plastic straw by 2020.[ccxxi] Of course there was some push back, and the most common thread was thinking that it was a small, mostly symbolic gesture, and that the city should have been focusing on the more pressing sewage and waste water problem that had bedeviled multiple administrations. Their point was that we should be fixing that big, hugely expensive problem instead of this seemingly small one. I understand how they might perceive this but I do not agree with their fundamental premise. Under this approach we should always be solving the biggest, most pressing and exigent problems and not the smaller, less dire problems, which actually vastly outnumber the big problems. In this manner we would never actually get to that silly problem of painting the park benches because there are always going to be far more "important" problems to solve. As communities we need to be able to do more than one thing at a time and solve many problems all at the same time—from the big, obvious ones to the small, hyper local, nearly invisible ones in our neighborhoods.

In the public health arena, there are some very interesting examples of such small but significant opportunities for change, including poor eyesight. According to a World Health Organization estimate, more than 1 billion people live with some form of vision impairment.[ccxxii] Their difficulties range from mild nearsightedness to blindness. Other estimates put the number even higher, at 2.5 billion people.[ccxxiii] Anything that negatively impacts a couple of *billion* people should rightly get people's attention, but because this seems like a mild problem compared to health crises such as AIDS or malaria, vision impairment receives far less attention. In fact, according to a 2016 World Economic Forum report, only $37 million was spent globally in 2015 on eye glasses—roughly two cents per person impacted.[ccxxiv] It is also estimated that for every year impaired vision goes untreated it costs the world more than $200 billion in lost productivity, all due to the lack of a simple pair of glasses.

The situation becomes even more alarming if we look beyond the direct economic impact. Children with poor eyesight don't do as well in school because most learning is still visual, and that feeds into lower literacy rates. Elderly people without glasses cannot read their medicine labels. They are more likely to become socially isolated, and isolation and loneliness are major factors in long term health. Drivers without glasses, particularly in the developing world, are having accidents that lead to injuries and fatalities. For adults everywhere, a pair of glasses means being more active and productive in all aspects of life.

Despite the obvious need and the incredibly simple solution that is readily available, funding—particularly from major philanthropic organizations—has not followed. Accord to the CEO of Essilor, France's largest eyeglass maker, when he pressed Bill Gates and the Gates Foundation about the notion of funding for eyeglasses, Gates indicated he had other priorities.[ccxxv] Of course, that is a reasonable answer, but one would think that Gates, as a computer engineer, might have an understanding of the power of recursion. Big problems and big projects occupy the lion's share of our attention and resources.

My point is that an investment in a small solution, repeated on a large scale (many times) would lead to the big solutions that Gates and others are working on. It just might not seem obvious at first and requires a different approach and mindset.

Another, less obvious example comes from the original twelve-step program, Alcoholics Anonymous. Alcoholics Anonymous, or AA, was started in Akron, Ohio, in 1935 by Bill Wilson and Dr. Bob Smith. Their support group approach was revolutionary at the time and became a model for many other programs in the 20th century. For those not familiar, AA has a simple structure: regularly scheduled meetings where people share stories, failures, and successes, along with the camaraderie of others who share their challenges. But the recursive part of AA is in the ritual of going to a meeting—that shared time and space makes the solution work.

I have known alcoholics. In fact, my mother was an alcoholic. She struggled with the disease all her life, but the longest stretch of her sobriety was when she was actively engaged in the AA program (in Akron, Ohio, no less). When someone is struggling, the first thing a fellow member will tell them is "Go to a meeting." It is not because the meeting itself is some magic bullet; rather, it brings those in need in contact with others who share their addiction and can help them through the hard times. The meetings themselves are ritualistic and follow a very predictable structure and agenda. You could walk into an AA meeting anywhere in the world, and it would be familiar.

AA also provides a social network for people who may have damaged their own network of friends and family. Do not underestimate the simple importance of a social connection, i.e., friends. Having someone to talk to, hang out with and, yes, hold you accountable, if need be. These program friends are how people relearn how to be social without a drink in their hand. They relearn the necessary skills of listening and relating to others. There is also the possibility of a professional network that people may leverage. Someone in the program knows someone who is looking for a roommate—connection made, and now someone has a place to live. Someone knows about a possible employment opportunity—connection made, and now someone has a steady job. These are all significant benefits that are ancillary to the main purpose of AA, yet they are a critical part of the overall success of the program.

Debates aside as to whether AA is as effective as other treatments for alcoholism, you cannot argue that it has worked for many, many people and has been doing so for decades. With nothing more than a room, chairs, donuts and lots of coffee, somehow this stripped-down program has been as successful as any other in treating the immense and complex problem of addiction.

Personal Recursion

I have been working on a bit of personal development this past year and have used a recursive solution to help facilitate my own growth. In an effort to be more open and present in my daily life and my relationships, I was doing a lot of soul searching on the subject. I would read, watch videos, listen to podcasts, and talk to some of my more enlightened friends—all of which certainly helped. However it was and has been a simple change that has had massive impact in my personal and professional life. I learned to walk slow.

I used to walk fast—very fast, actually. I would motor to and from my destinations and pat myself on the back for arriving so quickly. I would get impatient when walking behind people who were strolling along. I would be thinking, *C'mon, I gotta get somewhere!* I was actually putting a lot of stress on myself, and that fed into an overall anxiety. I was always pushing to get somewhere or get something done. This also manifested in my professional life, as anyone who has seen me speak over the past few years can attest—I also *talk* fast! In fact, people would often come up to me after a public talk and say that very thing. "Man do you talk fast!" I felt that I had so much information to share. I had to talk fast in order to get out everything I was thinking about.

In 2018, with a very conscious objective in mind, I began to walk slower. At first, it felt weird, but within a short period of time I seemed to adjust to the new pace. Then I started to notice more things on my walks. I saw a beautiful community garden adjacent to a senior living facility down the street from my house, which I had walked past dozens of times (apparently) yet never noticed. I saw new murals in my downtown. I said "hello" to more people, and I actually stopped and chatted with a few. My slow walk also gave me more time to think, which I believe helped me generate this book. It also carried over to my speaking and presentations. I even slowed down my talks. People may still say I talk fast, but for me it was a huge change in speed. I believe the talks got better as a result. In slowing down, I found new ideas to relay to my audiences, and content that I thought I knew backwards and forwards, began to take on new dimensions of meaning for me.

I started out the experiment with a specific goal and purpose. I found that my recursive solution not only got me to that goal, it opened up whole other dimensions, and gave me insight into other problems and challenges I never thought I could address. Instead of tackling the biggest problems, the highest profile or sexiest problems, what if we started with the small ones right in front of us? What if we started with the problems closest to us?

The Problems Closest to Us

As human beings sharing a small planet, we are interconnected in ways we don't even begin to perceive and comprehend. Collectively, we are facing huge challenges—climate change, global economic changes, and massive demographic and societal shifts—that will change the very foundations of our lives. Because these changes are so big and so difficult to see in the immediacy of our everyday experience, we actually feel them far less than even the most banal and mundane problems. We register climate change as a vast, existential problem, but how it manifests in our daily lives is less obvious. A storm seems stronger than before; the summer is hotter and drier; the winter feels different to us, but not completely unfamiliar. I believe this failure of perception is why we struggle to face the issue of climate change in more meaningful ways. It feels too remote to garner enough of our collective attention to inspire action. Sadly, that inaction may prove to be our undoing.

Why do we struggle to see the relatively small evidence that points to larger problems hidden right in front of us? Our radars, particularly when it comes to the idea of solving problems, generally home in on the big problem. We are taught to dream big, think big, go big or go home, and this has led to a type of functional blindness. We believe that we have to solve the big problem—that it is the only problem worth our time and our energy, and that solving a small problem is a denial of our gifts or our abilities. To do less is to squander a resource.

Recall our friend, Daniel Burnham, the famous planner and builder, and his most famous quote, "Make no little plans. They have no magic to stir men's blood and probably will not themselves be realized."

Bullshit.

After having been told by our parents, our teachers, our leaders, and our very culture that big is good and what we should strive for, is it any wonder that our radar only looks for big things? Yet, at heart, this goes against our human nature. What usually captures attention? It's the immediate problems that impact us here and now. These immediate problems, the problems that are closest to us, are the ones we feel the most acutely. If there's a pothole on your street, you notice it and you feel it. If the neighbors' yard hasn't been mowed in weeks, you cannot *not* see it. If the park where your kids play looks dirty and shabby, you've taken note. Global climate change is a huge problem and one that affects us all—but as I sit in my house or walk my neighborhood today, I just don't feel it.

What is interesting about small problems versus macro problems is that we tend to know how to fix small problems. We know where to start and we can actually be the ones who fix things, by going out and painting the park or lending our neighbors a hand and helping them mow the yard. That process of fixing something, of making something new or remaking something, is a tiny act of magic. It is a tiny act of creation.

I have written and spoken extensively on the idea of the love note—the relatively small change that has an outsized impact on the community. I used to think it was the love note itself that we should be paying attention to. Look at the project, look at the amazing result. Look at the people who did it. Those were the stories I told. Turns out, the love note is the thing that gets us to the thing. It is the making and doing of the love note that is the important part, not the end result. When we make, when we create, we summon forth something into the universe that did not exist before. It is in this energy that our creative and innovative persona resides. The recursion occurs *in us*. We manifest this energy, this magic trick of construction and, in doing so, we spark it in others. We become practiced, and the magic becomes easier and more comfortable to manifest. It becomes habit and even second nature. It changes us in a small way each time we do it. Over time, it can move mountains.

Perhaps it is only in hindsight that we can truly see the impact and significance of small, recursive acts. Just because they are hard to see in the moment does not mean we should not consciously try to create them. Let us look at these small acts as civic experiments. If they fail, we are likely out a small amount of time and resources. We will also have learned, I hope, from that failure. If the experiment succeeds only on the surface level, then we have painted some walls, planted some flowers, and done something nice and positive for the community. If we succeed in tapping into a recursive loop, then we begin what may be a series of experiments and interactions with far-reaching outcomes beyond what we imagined. The Broken Window Theory has entered our civic consciousness as a negative warning to cities about letting little instances of blight go untended. Let us find the "Painted Mailbox Theory" that leads us out of the fear and loss prevention side of communities and into the love, positive growth and aspirational side of our places.

Peter Kageyama

CHAPTER 9 – THE VALUE OF WHALES

In September 2017, Amazon dropped a proverbial bomb on cities across North America. The company announced that it would be seeking proposals for the location of its second corporate headquarters—or "HQ2," as the project became known widely—a venture that would entail $5 billion in new construction, funded by Amazon, and create an estimated 50,000 jobs in the host community. Cities in the U.S. and Canada scrambled to compete for the opportunity, submitting more than 200 applications.

Amazon's formal request for proposals (RFP) was surprisingly simple and brief, about four pages long. It included some basic criteria; the location needed to have a metro-area population of one million or more residents, a business-friendly environment, and logistics infrastructure including an international airport and interstate highway access. Despite its relatively simple terms, the document triggered a seismic impact among cities, some of which staged elaborate efforts to attract Amazon's attention. Kansas City (Missouri) mayor Sly James purchased 1,000 products on Amazon, which he then awarded 5-star reviews before donating to charity. New York City mayor Bill DeBlasio illuminated several city landmarks in Amazon orange to indicate the city's interest. The City of Stonecrest, Georgia, outside of Atlanta, voted to de-annex more than 300 acres of land and agreed to rename the area "Amazon, Georgia" for the corporate offices. Economic development offices everywhere kicked into high gear as teams struggled to assemble voluminous pitch packages for the October 2017 deadline. Most cities knew they had little chance of making the initial cut, let alone of winning the bid, but for a prize so big, they had to at least take a shot. Some officials told me they would use the process as a way of organizing community efforts and honing their pitches for a future major project that might come their way.

Not every city leapt at the opportunity. San Antonio Mayor Ron Nirenberg wrote a letter to Amazon CEO Jeff Bezos saying that his city would not be submitting a formal proposal. If the company decided to locate in San Antonio, the city would welcome Amazon, but "we're just not going to mortgage our future to do it," the mayor argued.[ccxxvi] Little Rock, Arkansas, made the gutsy move of preemptively 'breaking up' with Amazon and removing themselves from the competition. The city took out a one-page ad in the Jeff Bezos-owned *Washington Post*, declaring "It's not you (Amazon), it's us," adding that Little Rock and Amazon were just not a good fit. The ad garnered national attention, and Little Rock used the process to start a city-wide love campaign. (Of course, I approve of that!)

In January 2018, twenty cities were named to the list of finalists. Many were what you might call the usual suspects—New York City, Boston, Atlanta, and Washington, DC—major metropolitan areas that are already hubs for industry and talent magnets. But so, too, among the finalists were Columbus, Ohio; Miami, Florida; Toronto, Ontario; and Denver, Colorado (which I declared, in my last book, the next "it" city in America). There were interesting cases to be made for each place as a prospective site, and most of the cities—rightfully so—seemed to take making the top twenty as a badge of success.

During this process I heard from colleagues in these various cities that representatives had been quietly going to the survey each city as part of their process. So, while the final decision was being made in Seattle, the process spurred much discussion amongst cities and economic development professionals who were asking: Just how much would it take to entice Amazon to come to a region?

Clearly, Amazon was looking for more than just financial incentives, but everyone knew that financial incentives had to be part of the offer. How much would it take, ultimately? In 2017, the State of Wisconsin set the bar for incentives when they offered a total package worth $4.5 billion to Taiwanese electronics manufacturer Foxconn to bring some 13,000 jobs to the state. The estimated cost of each of these jobs was some $200,000 to the state, which was significantly more than the previous average of $12,400 for a new job created.[ccxxvii] Many argued that it would be decades before the state made money back on that investment.[ccxxviii] Everyone believed that the Amazon incentive package would be bigger, but just how much bigger?

As estimates on that number continued to grow and grow, there emerged significant backlash to this "Hunger Games"-style competition pitting communities against each other. Some, including noted urbanist Richard Florida, suggested that cities band together and pledge to not provide the estimated billions in economic incentives to the corporate giant.[ccxxix] That money could rightfully be spent on local infrastructure, education and many other social programs that would more directly impact their respective communities, went the argument—all of which was very true.

In November of 2018, Amazon made the historic and ultimately anti-climactic announcement that they would be splitting the new HQ into two separate locations—Northern Virginia just outside of Washington DC and New York City in the Long Island City neighborhood of Queens. Amazon cited the challenge of recruiting 50,000 skilled workers in any single location as a driving force behind the decision. Others noted that the new locations put Amazon in even tighter proximity to the political and financial centers of the United States. Regardless of the ultimate motivations, two infusions of 25,000+ jobs and billions of dollars of building and infrastructure would be seismic for those communities.

In New York it was revealed that Amazon would receive approximately $2.8 billion in incentives[ccxxx]. Virginia appears to have gotten a better deal with incentives of $573 million offered.[ccxxxi] Perhaps Amazon was giving a bit of a home town discount as CEO Jeff Bezos owns the Washington Post and spends considerable time there.

Many, especially in New York, were outraged—including the newly elected House member Alexandria Ocasio-Cortez, the Democratic-Socialist who represents parts of the

Queens community where Amazon would locate. Said Ocasio-Cortez "Amazon is a billion-dollar company…the idea that it will receive hundreds of millions of dollars in tax breaks at a time when our subway is crumbling and our communities need MORE investment, not less, is extremely concerning to residents here."[ccxxxii] One Democratic New York Assemblyman vowed to introduce legislation to cut the economic development budget and use those funds to lower student debt in the state. [ccxxxiii]

The negative reaction to the financial incentives is of course understandable. People will look at this and call it 'corporate welfare' and point to the obvious other needs their community has from crumbling infrastructure to underfunded social services.

Ocasio-Cortez and others quickly marshaled further support around this idea and Amazon was quickly put on the defensive in New York. On February 14, 2019, Amazon announced that it was withdrawing its decision to move to New York and would focus on Virginia and other regional opportunities.

Ocasio-Cortez took to Twitter to celebrate the decision. "Today was the day a group of dedicated, everyday New Yorkers and their neighbors defeated Amazon's corporate greed, its worker exploitation and the power of the richest man in the world,"[ccxxxiv] she wrote. Others, including New York Governor Andrew Cuomo called it a "lost economic opportunity"[ccxxxv] and noted that the politicians who opposed the deal should be held accountable. Time will ultimately tell and people will be comparing the two communities for years to come.

The actual levels of the incentives were significant but compared to what several others states offered, they were in fact kind of modest. Maryland offered the most at $8.5 billion, Newark & New Jersey offered $7 billion, and Pennsylvania offered $4.6 billion to locate in either Pittsburgh or Philadelphia.[ccxxxvi] Certainly incentives were a part of the final decision, but not the primary determinant. Amazon has to be able to recruit talent and New York City and Washington DC areas are already major talent magnets—a fact which seems to buttress the point discussed earlier, that "winner take all urbanism" benefits a small and increasingly select number of cities. Great for them, but for the vast majority of other places, it leaves them with a conundrum – how do we play this game? Or do we even want to play this game?

In the wake of the HQ2 process, communities everywhere are examining their economic development processes and asking hard questions. As the size and scope of the HQ2 process played out, and the estimated numbers and costs started to move into heretofore unseen (some would say, ridiculous) levels, citizens, business leaders, and even politicians started to ask questions about the process and the potential outcomes.

Communities are rightly seeking more information and transparency about just what their leaders are offering a company like Amazon. Think of it this way: Your city and its leadership are essentially committing your city (and, by extension, you) to a long-term relationship. Of course, we should be curious about just what the relationship means to us, because it will likely far outlive the terms of those who committed us to that marriage. Recall the Wisconsin deal with Foxconn and how it may take until the 2040s for the state to see a direct return on its initial investment.[ccxxxvii] Some cities have resisted these calls to disclose their bids[ccxxxviii] fearing, perhaps rightly so, that their communities would be shocked by what was being offered. If we look at the matter just through an economic lens, it is hard to justify extraordinary bargaining chips, especially when communities are faced with many other immediate, sometimes exigent, needs. But while the cost of an incentive may be outrageous, the value it eventually brings, which is often much harder to quantify, may be even greater. In economic development world, we count obvious metrics: jobs created, payroll taxes, incentives given, etc. We create a ledger and try to rationalize those numbers to our constituents and citizens. Sometimes that is hard to do. Certainly, the leadership in New York City and Virginia have the task of making the case to some in their community who stand aghast at the financial commitment that has been made to a generation of citizens. But this accounting method of measurement is, to my mind, insufficient to measure the actual impact—financial, environmental, physical and emotional—on a community.

To that end, I ask us to consider the possibility that, even with $5 billion in incentives and a cost of tens or even hundreds of thousands of dollars for each (projected) job created—the HQ2 project has been undervalued.

Understanding the economic development ecosystem

To understand better, I believe we should look at the question of such large companies, and how they affect us, not just through the lens of economic development but, rather, in terms of a biological event. Ask this question: What happens to an ecosystem when a "keystone species" changes?

The term keystone species was coined by zoologist Robert T. Paine in 1969 to define a species that has a disproportionately large impact on its ecosystem and plays a unique, even crucial, role in the function of that system. Many such keystone species are apex predators that dominate an ecosystem despite their relatively small numbers. Others are surprising species who somehow knit together and sustain complex webs of life. Depending on your point of view, and where you stand in the metaphorical food chain, Amazon is either an apex predator, such as a lion, or the less threatening elephant or whale, which massively impact the entire ecosystem without devouring everything in their path.

If we consider Amazon HQ2 in a biological framework, we begin to see how HQ2 will impact its community in many ways, some quite unexpected. This is because the introduction of HQ2 into its community will have huge ripples; in biological terms, it will be a "trophic cascade."

A trophic cascade is an event that starts at the top of the biosphere and cascades downward, impacting the entire food chain ecosystem along the way. Many of the resulting impacts are obvious and predictable, but many more are surprising, triggered by latent characteristics of the system, and sometimes more powerful than the more immediate, or expected, effects.

A fascinating example comes from Yellowstone National Park in the Western U.S. In the 1930s, the area's native grey wolf population was culled in a misguided effort to protect the local elk population. As a result, the elk population massively increased, in many ways surpassing the capacity of the environment to support it.[ccxxxix] Without natural predators, the elk had to move far less often, thus causing them to over-browse a location (i.e., to eat away excessively at vegetation such as shrubs). This depletion of plants and trees impacted the local beaver population, which fell to record lows by the 1990s. Fewer beavers meant fewer dams, which impacted many other species, as beavers are known as an 'engineer' species that creates niche ecosystems for many more creatures. You can see how the impact goes on and on.

In 1995, Yellowstone re-introduced the grey wolf to the park. Some immediate and obvious, arguably negative, impacts ensued—namely, the wolves killed some of the deer and elk. But they also changed the behavior of the deer and elk, causing them to move around more and, in some cases, to avoid areas that were conducive to being attacked. In turn, this allowed trees and plants to recover from over-browsing, which brought on an increase in beaver populations. Birds, reptiles, mice, rabbits and many more began to flourish again as balance was restored to the park. And something even more amazing happened; the rivers changed because of the wolves.

The depletion of trees and vegetation along the rivers had caused their banks to become less stable and more susceptible to erosion. The subsequent reduction in animal browsing and the increase in the beaver populations stabilized the riverbanks, thus physically changing the environment of the park. The return of the grey wolves as predators brought balance back to the entire park.[ccxl]

Another example, perhaps more relatable to Amazon, is that of the whale. Most of us learned in school how these massive creatures eat tons of fish and krill as they swim through the ocean. Some proponents of whaling, particularly in Japan, have used the seemingly logical argument that whaling makes room for other species to thrive and thus encourages more plant and animal life. In fact, the opposite turns out to be true—the decline of whales in our oceans has led to the diminishment fish and plankton and, ultimately, damaged our overall climate.[ccxli]

Yes, whales eat tons of fish and krill. But they also expel, in the form of waste, tons of nutrients into the ocean, particularly into the upper photosphere level, where light reaches into the ocean. It is here that ocean-based plants live, and photosynthesis occurs, which gives the krill and many other species something to eat. This photosynthesis also does something critical—it reduces the carbon dioxide in our breathable air. And it does so on such a massive scale that it is accurate to say that whales change the climate.[ccxlii] Turns out *Star Trek IV* was correct about the importance of whales!

If we consider Amazon HQ2 with the concepts of keystone species and trophic cascades in mind, we may begin to realize that there is likely far more to the company's impact than the number of jobs it creates, the money it spends on incentives or the resulting built infrastructure. What other entities will arise because of the presence of this keystone species? (Apartments, condominiums, banks, restaurants, shops, etc.) What physical elements will grow out of the presence of Amazon? (Parks, playgrounds, public squares, parking decks, roads, bridges, schools, etc.) What spinoffs will result, as talented people cycle into and out of Amazon? What other businesses will be attracted to the area because of HQ2 and its pool of talent? What philanthropic investments will Amazon and its beneficiaries make? Consider the three largest foundations in U.S.: The Bill & Melinda Gates Foundation, the Ford Foundation and the Getty Foundation. All of them stemmed from the success of the businesses created by their founders. Depending on the day and the current stock valuation, Amazon is one of the three most valuable companies on Earth, along with Apple and Microsoft. It is more valuable than General Motors, Ford Motor Company, and Exxon combined. What kind of foundation will Jeff Bezos set up once he decides to shift into the philanthropic phase of his career?

It is not farfetched to suggest that Amazon HQ2 may be the genesis of an urban growth curve the likes of which we have never seen before. The combination of urban locality, the size of the initial intervention, and the character of the company—one of the most valuable in the world and potentially the most significant company of the 21st century—make this a moon shot experiment and a gamble that two communities will undertake but every community will watch.

The Corporate Whale as Invasive Species

Clearly, I'm not a biologist—but bear with me as I take the biological analogy a step further. What if, instead of a trophic cascade, the corporate whales that cities often long to reel in have more in common with invasive species?

An invasive species has several characteristics reminiscent of Amazon: Fast growth, rapid reproduction, phenotype plasticity (the ability to alter form to suit changing conditions), the ability to sustain itself on multiple food sources, and an association/dependency with human beings.[ccxliii] Granted, your view of whether a corporation should be compared with an invasive species is likely to be influenced by where you sit on the economic food chain. Ask a local book store (if you can find one) about Amazon, and you may get an earful about the company's pernicious effects on smaller, traditional retail. We also see that now Amazon is proliferating into, and disrupting, some surprising industries—grocery stores, healthcare, and banking. Rapid reproduction, phenotype plasticity, wide range of food types? Check, check, check.

Is it possible that Amazon HQ2 will prove to more of a cancerous growth than an economic boon to its new host city? Absolutely. I recall folks in Reno, Nevada talking about the so-called "Tesla Effect" on their region after Tesla opened its huge "Gigafactory1" in 2016. The factory created over 2,500 new jobs as of late 2018[ccxliv], at a cost of $1.3 billion in economic incentives from the state. What has happened in Reno and the surrounding area is that housing prices have significantly increased and locals say that they are keenly aware of rising prices and a tightening housing market. Amazon's HQ2 is likely to have even more drastic impacts. I know someone who purchased a house in Northern Virginia just weeks before the announcement on the idea that if Amazon selected the region, his property value would immediately and

Peter Kageyama

significantly increase. Well played Todd… well played.

The HQ2 cities were selected in large part due to their physical, economic and educational infrastructure. Virginia will need to hope that their emotional infrastructure is just as strong. Success can be one of the most challenging of conditions and while they will be awash with the excitement of this new endeavor and this new relationship, they need to be cognizant that the growing pains of the next several years will be immense as well. Strong leadership will be required but so will patience, flexibility, and a sense of humility. It will be important to remember that feeling of winning, of accomplishment, because that will help carry through in tough times ahead. There is a great line from the 1981 film *Excalibur* where, following their great victory, Merlin warns King Arthur and his knights to "Savor it. Rejoice with great gladness. Remember this moment… for it is the doom of men that they forget."

There will be growing pains, many of them expected and predictable, such as increased property values, economic dislocation, and infrastructure stress. I am also certain there will be some negative externalities that we can't even imagine right now. Will these drawbacks outweigh the benefits of a massive investment like HQ2? History will make that determination. What is certain is that most of us already have a

266

relationship with Amazon—50% of households in the U.S. have Prime memberships[ccxlv]—and that relationship is growing increasingly deep and complex. Undeniably, Amazon already functions as a keystone species for billions of people across the developed world; if we perceive the company through this more complex and integrated lens, we will be better able to understand it, and its impact on our communities.

Peter Kageyama

CHAPTER 10 – CLOSING THOUGHTS

Much has happened since the publication of my first book *For the Love of Cities* in 2011. I thought it useful to update a few of the people and projects that I had written about previously.

Detroit has certainly come a long way since 2011. Once thought to be circling the drain, Detroit has showed its strength and character by rebounding into a modern success story. While far from perfect and far from done, Detroit and its many amazing people have brought that city back to a new life.

Claire Nelson was the founder of The Bureau of Urban Living, a small shop on Canfield Street in the Woodward corridor. I wrote about how she had been a retail pioneer in that neighborhood back in 2010/2011 and had encouraged others to come join the party. She certainly was successful, as the iconic Shinola store now resides just down the street from where Claire started. She has moved on to run the Urban Innovation Exchange and the Urban Consulate. The goal of both these groups is to share the best practices and knowledge of co-creators from around the city and around the country.

Phil Cooley, the co-creator and restaurateur who founded Slows BBQ in the Corktown neighborhood in 2005 has had an amazing trajectory. I first wrote about Phil in *For the Love of Cities* and talked about how Slows was a love note and a community anchor for the redevelopment of the Corktown neighborhood. *In Love Where You Live* (2015) I shared how he had bought an old industrial space and created Pony Ride, a 30,000 square foot space for other co-creators and entrepreneurs to make stuff. The space has been fully occupied for several years with 45 different tenants making up the community. Cooley's efforts to revitalize Corktown cannot be underestimated. Ford's acquisition of the Michigan Central Station (see chapter five) is the capstone on the turnaround in that neighborhood that Cooley and his friends started over a decade ago. Pony Ride is now in the midst of moving out of its current space[ccxlvi] and into an even bigger location in the Core City neighborhood,[ccxlvii] thus continuing the rebirth of the Motor City.

I am happy to report that Bob Devin Jones, creative director of the Studio @620 and the archetypal co-creator that I introduced in *For the Love of Cities* (and in fact used to literally define the category) is still going strong in St. Petersburg. The Studio @620 will celebrate 15 years in 2019. I would be remiss to not mention the passing of David Ellis, the other co-founder of the Studio, in 2018. David retired from the Studio several years ago, but his influence continues to be felt in the work they do and in the community as a whole.

I also highlighted a whimsical project called Swings Tampa Bay, which ran for a couple years in our community. Since then, co-founder Reuben Pressman has had a meteoric rise in the regional tech community. His startup, Presence, has received several rounds of venture funding and now employs more than 50 people in their downtown St. Petersburg offices. He was recently named "Entrepreneur in Residence" for the City of St. Petersburg by Mayor Rick Kriseman[ccxlviii].

In *For the Love of Cities*, I wrote about the heartache of LeBron James leaving Cleveland for Miami. I wrote at the time that "James will likely win championships in Miami, but I suspect they will not be as meaningful to him or to Miami as even a single championship would have meant to Cleveland."[ccxlix]

In 2014, at the conclusion of *Love Where You Live*, I again wrote about LeBron James—and his decision to return to his home in Ohio. The following year he led the Cavaliers and the entire city of Cleveland to the promised land by winning the NBA Championship and breaking a 50 year sports draught in Cleveland. And judging by the response that Cleveland had to that win, that one championship meant more to the city, and I believe to James as well, than any of the championships in Miami.

In 2018 James again left Cleveland for Los Angeles. What is significant is that his departure this time felt vastly different than in 2010. Certainly he handled the process better, but overall, fans—and really the entire city of Cleveland—handled the departure with a sense of equanimity and gratitude for what he had done. He fulfilled his promise and the hopes of an entire city. For that, Cleveland and all of us from Northeast Ohio will forever have nothing but love and respect for him and that team.

A couple of the love notes I wrote about in the first book are coming up on significant anniversaries. In Lexington, Kentucky, the "punk rock community marching band" March Madness celebrated 10 years together in 2018, and are still going strong. In Providence, Rhode Island, Waterfire, the amazing community ritual and tradition created by Barnaby

Evans, will celebrate 25 years in 2019. Always spectacular, I imagine Evans and the Waterfire team will find new and innovative ways of showcasing the city and their signature event.

Return to Lake Eola

Lake Eola, the psychic center of the city of Orlando, served as a backdrop for an event that no one wanted. In the early morning hours of June 12, 2016, the Pulse Nightclub in Orlando became the scene of America's worst mass shooting to date. Forty-nine people were killed by a deranged gunman in a horrific explosion of hate, terrorism, religious fanaticism, and geopolitics. The shooting was also the largest attack on the LGBTQ community in American history. The city—in fact the entire nation—reeled from this act. In the immediate aftermath of shooting, Mayor Dyer and the City of Orlando's commitment to rebuilding the fountain at Lake Eola would prove to be a key piece of the community's emotional infrastructure.

On Monday, June 13, 2016 a grass roots vigil began to take shape. Organized not by the city, but by a small group of people, word spread rapidly through social media and some official channels. They had no idea how many people might show up. Mayor Dyer told me "there's ten thousand, twenty thousand, thirty thousand, forty thousand, people that came out. It was extremely, extremely emotional. And then, before it started, it wasn't even raining, but a rainbow formed behind the band shell. It's unbelievable that that occurred. I think it was a good healing for the city."

Lake Eola and the fountain, the emotional and psychic center of the community, became the place where people instinctively gathered in a time of extreme sadness and crisis. The emotional infrastructure of our places is not just there to please the eyes and make us feel better about our cities. Emotional infrastructure is there when we literally want to fall to our knees and weep or scream in pain and anger. I hope that your city never has to face a situation like Orlando did, but sadly we know this will happen again. It must now be part of our placemaking to consider this question of where will we gather to celebrate, where will we gather to mourn?

In the aftermath of shooting, the city found itself returning to the lake and the imagery of the fountain because of its emotional resonance. Heather Fagan, the Deputy Chief of Staff for Mayor Dyer said, "We made a graphic of the fountain and made a rainbow color right after Pulse. And that sort of became the symbol that was used throughout everything that we did and that everyone did. The fountain… became the iconic symbol of healing and unity."

The fountain also became the new symbol of the city. Orlando changed its logo to the image of the fountain and even changed the city's flag in 2017.[ccl] In early 2017, the city launched a design contest for the new flag and the winner was again the iconic image of the fountain. Tragedy brought the community together and when they came together in the heart of their community, that piece of emotional infrastructure supported them in their time of need, and reminds them of their strength and resilience moving forward.

Long live Orlando.

A final thought - Cherish your Co-creators

I have been sharing the idea of the co-creator to communities all over the world. It has been a notion that seems to resonate wherever I share it because it's is one of the universal truths in our cities and places. Every city has its co-creators, those people who shave activated their love of their place and put that into action. Once I point out what they are and what they do, people recognize them in their own community. Yeah, I know that person! Yes, that sounds like what Bob does here or Jane does there. We know, and I do believe appreciate, our co-creators but I now believe we need to do more for them.

Peter Kageyama

As part of my work with leadership in places I am usually asked what we as the city/county/place do to support the co-creators in our midst? I outlined a simple process in *Love Where You Live* where city leaders identify their major co-creators, invite them for a conversation, learn about what they are already doing, and see how they might align that with what the city is doing. Dialog that hopefully leads to communication. I now have something else for city leadership to consider.

By giving a name to this group of people in every community, we have helped cities to identify them. If we know who they are or who we are looking for, we can work with them. Simple enough. Cities must also be very careful in their everyday dealings with these co-creators. Some may not actually want to play with you. They have their own vision and their own process, and for the most part they look at officials as obstacles. Cities need to respect that. You are better off knowing what these co-creators are doing and perhaps adjusting your own efforts around them. That seems extraordinary for most cities as they are used to the idea of leading and calling the shots. A smart city will know when to get in the backseat and let someone else drive. Even smarter cities will understand how to say no in the right way.

Because these co-creators are moving fast and following their passions and creative instincts, they are very likely not doing this exactly the way that the city, or more specifically, the city attorney or code enforcement officials might like them to do it. This will be a real challenge for many city leaders as control is very hard to cede, especially when you know that often times the rules and the code are in place for good reasons: health, safety, etc. So, sometimes a you may have to say no to these co-creators and their work. But in saying no to them you will need to understand something. You think you are saying no to an activity - "you can't have an open flame in here" or "that venue just cannot hold 200 people." You're saying 'no' to an activity for what is likely a sound reason. What these co-creators hear, and feel is that you are saying "no" to who they are as people. These are people who are going above and beyond ordinary levels of citizenship and trying to create something new and valuable. They are going to feel highly connected to the work and your 'no', even for good reasons, is going to feel like a negation of their very identity. And if you say 'no' to them multiple times, they are very likely to lose interest and lose hope. So, to all of you city and community leaders out there, know this—you need to cherish your co-creators. This does not mean that you will bless and allow all their crazy work, but it does mean that you will think about how you treat them, and when you tell them 'no,' you do it with sensitivity. Most importantly, recognize that these people are the most important emotional infrastructure in all our cities.

These people are the heroes of the stories, they are the innovators and the difference makers. They are the shining light on the hill that calls us all towards a better community, a better way and even our better selves. Love lives at that light on the hill and it is my hope that we all find our way there.

ABOUT THE AUTHOR

Peter Kageyama is the author of *For the Love of Cities: The Love Affair Between People and Their Places,* the follow up, *Love Where You Live: Creating Emotionally Engaging Places,* and the latest, *The Emotional Infrastructure of Places.* Peter is a Senior Fellow with the Alliance for Innovation, a national network of city leaders and a special advisor to America In Bloom.

Known as "The City Love Guy," he has also been called "the best friend of cities" as he relentlessly looks for the positive and the good in every place he visits. He is the former President of Creative Tampa Bay, a grassroots community change organization and the co-founder of the Creative Cities Summit, an interdisciplinary conference that brings citizens and practitioners together around the big idea of 'the city.

He is an internationally sought-after community development consultant and grassroots engagement strategist who speaks all over the world about bottom-up community development and the amazing people who are making change happen.

He lives in St. Petersburg, Florida and is a proud dog parent to Buffy, Finney and Dobby.

Peter Kageyama

ENDNOTES

[i] http://money.cnn.com/2017/03/09/news/infrastructure-report-card/index.html

[ii] http://www.cnn.com/2013/07/16/tech/innovation/elon-musk-tube-transport/index.html

[iii] https://www.citylab.com/transportation/2016/04/how-columbus-is-using-transit-to-reduce-infant-mortality/480213/

[iv] https://www.citylab.com/transportation/2017/11/when-a-smart-city-doesnt-have-all-the-answers/542976/

[v] http://www.nacsonline.com/About_NACS/Pages/default.aspx

[vi] Time, October 23, 2017 – Electric vehicles are here. Now we need to figure out how to charge them. Justin Worland

[vii] https://www.scientificamerican.com/article/the-u-s-has-1-million-electric-vehicles-but-does-it-matter/

[viii] https://www.nanalyze.com/2017/03/electric-cars-usa/

[ix] http://www.theenergycollective.com/energy-innovation-llc/2413425/americas-electric-vehicle-future-part-1-65-75-light-duty-vehicle-sales-2050

[x] https://electrek.co/2017/07/04/electric-car-norway-tesla-model-x/

[xi] https://www.nbcnews.com/mach/tech/electric-car-revolution-may-come-sooner-we-thought-ncna780516

[xii] https://www.cnbc.com/2017/04/10/tesla-passes-general-motors-to-become-the-most-valuable-us-automaker.html

[xiii] https://www.engadget.com/2017/12/17/tesla-discourages-commercial-cars-from-using-superchargers/

[xiv] https://electrek.co/2017/06/19/us-electric-vehicle-charging-stations/

[xv] http://www.latimes.com/business/autos/la-fi-hy-ev-charging-stations-20171218-story.html

[xvi] Ibid

[xvii] http://www.pewinternet.org/fact-sheet/internet-broadband/

[xviii] http://muniwireless.com/2009/09/28/st-cloud-shuts-down-free-citywide-wifi-service/

xix https://venturebeat.com/2019/03/28/linknycs-6-million-users-have-downloaded-8-6-terabytes-of-data/

xx
http://www.crainsnewyork.com/article/20170215/TECHNOLOGY/170219939/after-controversy-linknyc-wi-fi-kiosks-have-been-gaining-popularity

xxi https://nypost.com/2016/06/19/horny-homeless-men-use-times-square-wi-fi-to-watch-porn/

xxii https://www.dnainfo.com/new-york/20160711/upper-east-side/linknyc-kiosks-clogging-sidewalks-with-encampments-drug-deals-locals

xxiii Ibid

xxiv https://venturebeat.com/2019/03/28/linknycs-6-million-users-have-downloaded-8-6-terabytes-of-data/

xxv https://www.statista.com/statistics/283334/global-average-selling-price-smartphones/

xxvi https://www.recode.net/2017/10/24/16527600/smartphone-price-around-the-world-apple-samsung-huawei

xxvii http://www.pewinternet.org/fact-sheet/mobile/

xxviii Ibid

xxix
https://motherboard.vice.com/en_us/article/ezpk77/chattanooga-gigabit-fiber-network

xxx Ibid

xxxi https://www.cbsnews.com/news/fastest-internet-service-in-us-found-in-an-unlikely-city/

xxxii http://ftpcontent2.worldnow.com/wrcb/pdf/091515EPBFiberStudy.pdf

xxxiii https://muninetworks.org/communitymap

xxxiv Ibid

xxxv http://www.coloradoan.com/story/news/2017/05/31/comcast-beats-fort-collins-punch-gigabit-internet-service/355531001/

xxxvi http://www.coloradoan.com/story/news/2017/10/25/election-committee-raises-200-k-fight-fort-collins-broadband-issue/799292001/

xxxvii https://muninetworks.org/content/local-authority-wins-across-colorado-comcast-loses-fort-collins

xxxviii http://www.coloradoan.com/story/opinion/2017/10/20/our-view-cautious-yes-fort-collins-broadband/756643001/

xxxix http://www.nytimes.com/2013/03/14/business/energy-environment/cities-weigh-taking-electricity-business-from-private-utilities.html

xl http://www.denverpost.com/2017/10/27/boulder-wanted-its-own-electric-utility-does-it-still/

xli http://www.dailycamera.com/boulder-election-news/ci_31439744/boulder-municipalization-persists-after-surprise-election-comeback

xlii https://en.wikipedia.org/wiki/Natural_monopoly

xliii https://www.fastcompany.com/3059527/poor-areas-of-cities-have-really-terrible-mobile-service

xliv https://www.politico.com/magazine/story/2015/02/harvey-milks-first-crusade-dog-poop-114811_Page2.html

xlv https://www.avma.org/KB/Resources/Statistics/Pages/Market-research-statistics-US-pet-ownership.aspx

xlvi https://www.statista.com/statistics/414956/dog-population-european-union-eu-by-country/

xlvii http://www.businessinsider.com/japan-has-more-registered-pets-than-it-has-children-2014-5

xlviii http://www.pijac.org/sites/default/files/pdfs/2014T2TpptRichter.pdf

xlix http://www.adweek.com/brand-marketing/44-of-millennials-see-their-pets-as-starter-children-and-thats-a-big-opportunity-for-brands/

l https://www.washingtonpost.com/news/business/wp/2016/09/13/millennials-are-picking-pets-over-people

li http://blogs.seattletimes.com/fyi-guy/2013/02/01/in-seattle-its-cats-dogs-and-kids-in-that-order/

lii https://thebolditalic.com/san-francisco-dogs-by-the-numbers-the-bold-italic-san-francisco-dd1b09798142 liii https://www.news4jax.com/sports/jacksonville-jaguars-adding-instadium-dog-park

liv https://www.entrepreneur.com/article/292682

lv
http://www.humanesociety.org/news/press_releases/2010/08/benefits_of_dogs_at_work_081710.html

lvi http://newsstand.clemson.edu/clemson-research-suggests-parks-and-green-spaces-can-reduce-crime/

lvii http://time.com/9912/10-things-your-commute-does-to-your-body/

lviii Ibid ii

lix https://mobility.tamu.edu/ums/report/

lx Stress That Doesn't Pay: The Commuting Paradox – Stutzer & Frey, 2004, http://ftp.iza.org/dp1278.pdf

lxi The Exploding Metropolis, William H. Whyte Jr. Are Cities Un-American, page 12, Doubleday 1958

lxii http://exchange.aaa.com/wp-content/uploads/2015/04/Your-Driving-Costs-2015.pdf

lxiii http://www.latimes.com/business/autos/la-fi-hy-millennials-cars-20161223-story.html

lxiv
https://www.washingtonpost.com/news/business/wp/2017/02/28/the-surprising-reason-some-millennials-may-be-buying-new-cars/

lxv https://disneyinstitute.com/blog/2012/06/what-time-is-the-3-oclock-parade/

lxvi https://blog.smarking.net/visualizing-seasonal-parking-demand-cdda5c5c8b86

lxvii https://blog.smarking.net/travel-demand-management-at-its-finest-6252a614228d

lxviii https://blog.smarking.net/travel-demand-management-at-its-finest-6252a614228d

lxix https://blog.smarking.net/just-when-you-thought-parking-in-aspen-couldnt-get-any-better-1695a2dd7c73

lxx https://blog.smarking.net/just-when-you-thought-parking-in-aspen-couldnt-get-any-better-1695a2dd7c73

lxxi Linda Clarke (2002). Building Capitalism (Routledge Revivals): Historical Change and the Labour Process in the Production of Built

Environment. Routledge. p. 115.

lxxii http://www.pedbikeinfo.org/planning/facilities_bike_bikelanes.cfm

lxxiii http://detroitgreenways.org; Say Hello to the Mobility City, Todd Scott, June 22, 2018

lxxiv http://www.crainsdetroit.com/article/20180617/opinion01/663806/keith-crain-say-goodbye-to-the-motor-city

lxxv http://www.tampabay.com/news/City-rejects-bike-lanes-on-Bay-to-Bay-suggesting-neighborhood-streets-instead_166975594

lxxvi http://www.tampabay.com/news/City-rejects-bike-lanes-on-Bay-to-Bay-suggesting-neighborhood-streets-instead_166975594

lxxvii https://jointventure.org/initiatives/mobility/managers-mobility-partnership

lxxviii https://international.kk.dk/sites/international.kk.dk/files/turist_info_2018_a4.pdf

lxxix https://www.limebike.com/blog/lime-smart-mobility-backed-by-gv-uber

lxxx https://techcrunch.com/2018/04/09/uber-acquires-bike-share-startup-jump/

lxxxi https://www.independent.co.uk/news/uk/home-news/is-this-the-future-of-transport-9222902.html

lxxxii https://www.denverpost.com/2018/06/01/denver-electric-scooter-removal/

lxxxiii https://www.tennessean.com/story/news/2018/05/31/bird-scooters-nashville-sweeps-remove-public-way/659745002/

lxxxiv https://www.independent.co.uk/news/uk/home-news/is-this-the-future-of-transport-9222902.html

lxxxv https://finance.yahoo.com/news/9-plaintiffs-suing-e-scooter-industry-201804356.html

lxxxvi https://www.cnet.com/news/bird-goes-after-helmet-laws-for-electric-scooters/

lxxxvii Time Magazine, October 15, 2018 pg. 39

lxxxviii https://www.fs.fed.us/nrs/pubs/jrnl/2015/nrs_2015_kondo_004.pdf

lxxxix Ibid

xc https://www.citylab.com/solutions/2016/04/vacant-lots-green-space-crime-research-statistics/476040/

xci Ibid

xciihttps://web.archive.org/web/20100612233532/http://millenniu
mpark.org/newsandmedia/pdfs/4.1%20Millennium%20Park%20Aw
ards.pdf

xciii

https://www.nrpa.org/uploadedFiles/nrpaorg/Professional_Develo
pment/Innovation_Labs/Power-of-Parks-Study-Chicago-Park-
District.pdf

xciv https://www.cityparksalliance.org/why-urban-parks-
matter/economic-value

xcv http://newsstand.clemson.edu/clemson-research-suggests-parks-
and-green-spaces-can-reduce-crime/

xcvi https://www.nrpa.org/our-work/Three-Pillars/social-equity-and-
parks-and-recreation/

xcvii https://wsbt.com/news/local/south-bend-man-is-helping-the-
community-by-fixing-peoples-bikes

xcviii https://nrf.com/resources/retail-library/the-economic-impact-
of-the-us-retail-industry

xcix http://ec.europa.eu/growth/single-market/services/retail_en

c https://ilsr.org/key-studies-why-local-matters/

ci https://papers.ssrn.com/sol3/papers.cfm?abstract_id=2540321

cii http://www.wglt.org/post/downtown-areas-can-be-model-
economic-development#stream/0

ciii Daniel Okrent (2003). Great Fortune: The Epic of Rockefeller
Center. New York: Viking Press. pp. 246–7.

civ Davis, *Jews And Booze: Becoming American In The Age Of Prohibition*, p.
191.

cv https://www.theatlantic.com/business/archive/2018/01/german-
board-games-catan/550826/

cvi https://www.usatoday.com/story/life/2017/07/31/bored-digital-
games-join-board-game-renaissance/476986001/

cvii

https://www.businesswire.com/news/home/20161228005057/en/T
op-3-Trends-Impacting-Global-Board-Games

cviii Freehill-Maye, Lynn (2016-01-26). "In Toronto Cafes Board

Games Rule". *The New York Times.*

cix The Customer Experience of Town Centres; Cathy Hart, Loughborough University Leicestershire, UK , 2014
cxhttp://www.slate.com/articles/business/metropolis/2017/04/the_retail_apocalypse_is_suburban.html
cxi https://ilsr.org/key-studies-why-local-matters/#3
cxii https://www.huffingtonpost.com/diana-mackie/marketing-success-with-local-pride_b_7036870.html
cxiii ibid
cxiv https://offices.net/report-washington-state.htm
cxv http://www.tbo.com/news/business/owner-fuses-downtown-tampa-coffee-bar-with-real-estate-agent-hub-20160916/
cxvi ibid

cxvii Lost Detroit: Stories Behind the Motor City's Majestic Ruins, Dan Austin, History Press, 2010

cxviiihttps://www.freep.com/story/money/cars/ford/2018/09/24/matty-moroun-michigan-central-station/1412930002/
cxix http://www.standard.net/Guest-Commentary/2018/04/24/Sears-Newgate-Mall-retailers-Amazon-internet-disruption-column-Ferro
cxx http://articles.sun-sentinel.com/1991-02-15/business/9101080852_1_wal-mart-stores-supercenter-stores-hypermart-usa-units
cxxi https://www.usatoday.com/story/money/2018/10/15/sears-bankruptcy/1595399002/
cxxii https://www.chicagotribune.com/business/ct-biz-sears-bankruptcy-buys-time-20190116-story.html
cxxiii Jamestown's Michael Phillips on Ponce City Market", ATL Food Chatter (Atlanta magazine blog), July 18, 2011

cxxivhttps://web.archive.org/web/20120326123104/http://www.atlantamagazine.com/covereddish/diningnews/blogentry.aspx?BlogEntryID=10261127
cxxv https://www.hotspotrentals.com/hottest-neighborhoods-america/

cxxvi https://www.youtube.com/watch?v=5KH2314st2U
CityAge.TV: Keynote by Todd Richardson, Director, Sears
Crosstown Development (Memphis, TN)
cxxvii https://www.youtube.com/watch?v=5KH2314st2U
CityAge.TV: Keynote by Todd Richardson, Director, Sears
Crosstown Development (Memphis, TN)

cxxviii https://www.popsci.com/repurposing-big-box-stores#page-2
cxxix https://www.usatoday.com/story/money/nation-
now/2018/06/24/toys-r-us-all-stores-closing-june-29/728636002/
cxxx https://www.clevescene.com/scene-and-
heard/archives/2017/07/20/an-amazon-fulfillment-center-could-
bring-life-back-to-former-randall-park-mall-site
cxxxi https://www.ohio.com/akron/news/local/is-amazon-moving-
into-former-rolling-acres-mall-site
cxxxii http://www.mcallenlibrary.net/about/newmain
cxxxiii
https://www.freep.com/story/money/business/2017/11/27/empty
-big-box-stores-michigan/830459001/
cxxxiv https://medium.com/agrilyst/lets-talk-about-market-size-
316842f1ab27
cxxxv
https://www.detroitnews.com/story/business/2016/08/15/indoor-
farms-vacant-buildings-detroit/88813972/
cxxxvi
https://www.desertsun.com/story/money/business/2018/05/11/la
rge-cannabis-cultivation-cathedral-city-denied/593126002/

cxxxvii
https://www.desertsun.com/story/money/business/2018/05/11/la
rge-cannabis-cultivation-cathedral-city-denied/593126002/

cxxxviii http://www.modernphoenix.net/beefeaters.htm
cxxxix http://www.eastvalleytribune.com/money/jay-newton-s-beef-
eaters-property-up-for-sale/article_5845feaa-3045-573b-b24a-
3478287be946.html

---

cxl https://www.hgbhealth.com/about-hgb/alive
cxli https://www.supermarketnews.com/retail-amp-financial/spartan-pay-385-million-felpausch
cxlii http://www.wbaa.org/post/whom-bell-tolls-after-20-year-effort-crawfordsville-gets-clock-tower-back#stream/0
cxliii https://www.youtube.com/watch?v=ckqNCb8oMy0
cxliv https://youtu.be/e4_Xv7Rsz88
cxlv
https://www.starbucks.com/assets/ba6185aa2f9440379ce0857d89de8412.pdf
cxlvi https://www.steelcase.com/research/articles/topics/design-q-a/q-ray-oldenburg/
cxlvii http://tcbmag.com/news/articles/2018/february/target-remains-top-employer-in-downtown-minneapoli
cxlviii https://corporate.target.com/article/2012/10/target-plaza-commons-beyond-the-breakroom
cxlix https://corporate.target.com/article/2012/11/office-envy-the-unveiling-of-target-plaza-commons
cl https://www.steelcase.com/research/articles/topics/design-q-a/q-ray-oldenburg/
cli https://www.seattletimes.com/business/amazon/take-a-look-inside-amazons-spheres-as-they-get-set-for-next-weeks-opening/
clii https://www.seattletimes.com/business/amazon/amazons-spheres-are-centerpiece-of-4-billion-effort-to-transform-seattles-urban-core/
cliii https://www.nytimes.com/2018/12/12/travel/checking-in-no-thanks-im-just-here-to-use-the-wi-fi.html
cliv http://moxy-hotels.marriott.com/en/our-story
clv https://www.nytimes.com/2018/12/12/travel/checking-in-no-thanks-im-just-here-to-use-the-wi-fi.html
clvi https://www.nzherald.co.nz/bay-of-plenty-times/news/article.cfm?c_id=1503343&objectid=12108574
clvii https://www.tampabay.com/business/st-pete-piers-official-budget-is-80-million-but-other-pots-providing-millions-more-20190114/
clviii The Happy City, Charles Montgomery
clix https://www.citylab.com/transportation/2018/08/is-this-americas-nicest-bus-station/567392/

clx https://www.sfchronicle.com/bayarea/article/Salesforce-buys-naming-rights-to-Transbay-Transit-11274011.php

clxi *The New Urban Crisis: How Our Cities Are Increasing Inequality, Deepening Segregation, And Failing The Middle-Class – And What We Can Do About It*, Richard Florida, Basic Books, 2017, pg 6.

clxii https://www.youtube.com/watch?v=S9ry1M7JlyE

clxiii http://www.city-journal.org/2015/25_4_gentrification.html - Kay S. Hymowitz

clxiv https://www.citylab.com/equity/2015/09/the-role-of-public-investment-in-gentrification/403324/

clxv http://insideairbnb.com/venice/

clxvi http://www.telegraph.co.uk/travel/news/tempers-flare-in-venice-as-angry-protesters-block-cruise-ships/

clxvii https://theculturetrip.com/europe/italy/articles/science-says-this-is-when-venice-will-become-an-underwater-city/

clxviii https://www.ferdamalastofa.is/static/files/ferdamalastofa/Fretta myndir/2018/oktober/tourism-in-iceland-2018.pdf

clxix https://grapevine.is/news/2018/10/18/icelands-tourism-minister-calls-for-tourist-limits/

clxx http://nymag.com/daily/intelligencer/2014/02/spike-lee-amazing-rant-against-gentrification.html

clxxi https://www.huffingtonpost.com/entry/a-new-generation-of-anti-gentrification-radicals-are-on-the-march-in-los-angeles-and-around-the-country_us_5a9d6c45e4b0479c0255adec

clxxii Ibid xiii

clxxiii https://whyy.org/articles/point-breeze-developer-claims-arson-is-part-of-backlash-against-gentrification/

clxxiv Ibid xiii

clxxv https://www.citylab.com/equity/2017/03/the-neighborhood-that-went-to-war-against-gentrifiers/518181/

clxxvi http://www.lamag.com/citythinkblog/guillermo-uribe-on-the-gentrification-of-east-l-a/

clxxvii https://www.citylab.com/equity/2016/08/defining-gentefication-in-latino-neighborhoods/495923/

clxxviii http://www.lamag.com/guillermo-uribe-on-the-gentrification-of-east-l-a/

clxxix Ibid ix

clxxx Gentrification, displacement and the arts: Untangling the relationship between arts industries and place change; Carl Grodach, Nicole Foster, James Murdoch, First Published December 6, 2016
https://doi.org/10.1177/0042098016680169
clxxxi Richard Florida, https://www.citylab.com/life/2018/03/do-art-scenes-really-lead-to-gentrification/556208/
clxxxii Richard Florida, https://www.citylab.com/life/2018/03/do-art-scenes-really-lead-to-gentrification/556208/
clxxxiii "Physicist, Purge Thyself" in the *Chicago Tribune Magazine* (22 June 1969)

clxxxiv https://highline.huffingtonpost.com/articles/en/poor-millennials/
clxxxv https://www.washingtonpost.com/national/health-science/us-life-expectancy-declines-for-the-first-time-since-1993/2016/12/07/7dcdc7b4-bc93-11e6-91ee-1adddfe36cbe_story.html?utm_term=.c221fa38e056; December 8, 2016 Lenny Bernstein
clxxxvi Ibid viii
clxxxvii Lee, Ellen (1 March 2011). "Airbnb passes bookings: 1 million nights". *San Francisco Chronicle.*

clxxxviii Wauters, Robin (26 January 2012). "Airbnb: 5 Million Nights Booked, Opening 6 New International Offices In Q1 2012". *TechCrunch.*

clxxxix https://www.recode.net/2017/7/19/15949782/airbnb-100-million-stays-2017-threat-business-hotel-industry
cxc https://www.politico.com/states/f/?id=00000161-44f2-daac-a3e9-5ff3d8740001
cxci https://www.airbnbcitizen.com/correcting-flawed-studys-false-assertions-community/
cxcii https://ny.curbed.com/2018/1/30/16950424/airbnb-gentrification-nyc-median-rent-study
cxciii https://nextcity.org/daily/entry/seattle-airbnb-tax-displacement
cxciv https://nextcity.org/daily/entry/boston-joins-other-cities-in-limiting-airbnb-rentals

cxcv https://grapevine.is/news/2018/06/21/airbnb-in-iceland-growing-fast-driving-up-costs-mostly-not-registered-legally/
cxcvi https://grapevine.is/news/2017/11/23/icelands-capital-losing-millions-from-illegal-airbnb-listings/

cxcvii https://nextcity.org/daily/entry/airbnb-gets-housing-wrong
cxcviii http://www.tampabay.com/news/transportation/uber-lyft-rules-to-get-hearing-in-hillsborough-but-no-final-resolution-yet/2293482
cxcix

cc https://www.hotelmanagement.net/own/continued-growth-projected-for-u-s-hotel-industry-2018
cci http://news.cornell.edu/stories/2017/10/hotels-thrive-even-age-airbnb
ccii https://www.marketwatch.com/story/bed-and-breakfasts-are-holding-fast-in-the-age-of-airbnb-and-expedia-2016-09-08
cciii Maureen Kennedy, Paul Leonard (April 2001). "Dealing with Neighborhood Change: A Primer on Gentrification and Policy Choices". The Brookings Institution Center on Urban and Metropolitan Policy and PolicyLink.

cciv NYU Furman Center for Real Estate and Urban Policy, *State of New York City's Housing and Neighborhoods in 2015,* May 2016, http://furmancenter.org/files/sotc/NYUFurmanCenter_SO_Cin2015_9JUNE2016.pdf
ccv
http://journals.sagepub.com/doi/abs/10.1177/1078087404273341
ccvi Ibid xxi
ccvii Florida, Richard, The New Urban Crisis (2016), p71
ccviii https://www.washingtonpost.com/opinions/five-myths-about-gentrification/2016/06/03/b6c80e56-1ba5-11e6-8c7b-6931e66333e7_story.html
ccix http://austincouncilforum.org/viewtopic.php?f=2&t=1076&sid=8ecb31a28b9255ca212680b652792ee9
ccx http://austincouncilforum.org/viewtopic.php?f=2&t=1076&sid=8ecb31a28b9255ca212680b652792ee9
ccxi https://www.austinchronicle.com/news/2019-04-19/public-notice-two-steps-forward/

ccxii Ibid v

ccxiii https://fivethirtyeight.com/features/the-most-diverse-cities-are-often-the-most-segregated/

ccxiv https://www.youtube.com/watch?v=TWKPtw6a8_g

ccxv https://nextcity.org/features/view/how-this-philadelphia-neighborhood-is-gentrifying-without-displacement

ccxvi "Recursion." *Merriam-Webster.com*. Merriam-Webster, n.d. Web. 10 Aug. 2018.

ccxvii http://www.ecocycle.org/bestrawfree/faqs

ccxviii https://www.nytimes.com/2018/05/01/travel/straw-bans-hotels-resorts.html

ccxix https://www.usatoday.com/story/news/2018/07/18/anti-straw-movement-based-unverified-statistic-500-million-day/750563002/

ccxx https://www.usatoday.com/story/news/world/2018/04/19/britain-plans-ban-plastic-straws-cotton-swabs/532028002/

ccxxi https://www.tampabay.com/st-petersburg/st-petersburg-to-vote-on-straw-ban-20181213/

ccxxii https://www.nytimes.com/2018/05/05/health/glasses-developing-world-global-health.html

ccxxiii http://www3.weforum.org/docs/WEF_2016_EYElliance.pdf

ccxxiv http://www3.weforum.org/docs/WEF_2016_EYElliance.pdf

ccxxv https://www.nytimes.com/2018/05/05/health/glasses-developing-world-global-health.html

ccxxvi http://time.com/4987883/amazon-hq2-headquarters-costs/

ccxxvii http://cepr.net/blogs/cepr-blog/scott-walker-foxconn-and-the-wisconsin-economic-development-corporation

ccxxviii Ibid

ccxxix https://www.cnn.com/2018/01/20/opinions/amazon-headquarters-competition-disturbing-richard-florida-opinion/index.html

ccxxx https://ny.curbed.com/2018/11/16/18098589/amazon-hq2-nyc-queens-long-island-city-explained

ccxxxi https://www.washingtonpost.com/local/virginia-news/amazon-hq2-to-receive-more-than-28-billion-in-incentives-from-virginia-new-york-and-tennessee/2018/11/13/f3f73cf4-e757-11e8-a939-9469f1166f9d_story.html?noredirect=on&utm_term=.a21672825d04

ccxxxii https://www.huffingtonpost.com/entry/amazon-hq2-jeff-bezos-new-york-politicians-letter_us_5beb07bde4b044bbb1a9927e

ccxxxiii https://capitalandmain.com/will-new-york-fund-amazon-subsidies-or-student-debt-relief-1113

ccxxxiv https://www.yahoo.com/news/alexandria-ocasio-cortez-celebrated-amazon-210337989.html

ccxxxv https://www.governor.ny.gov/news/statement-governor-andrew-m-cuomo-196

ccxxxvi https://triblive.com/local/allegheny/14289172-74/gov-tom-wolf-says-pennsylvania-offered-46b-in-incentives-for-amazon

ccxxxvii http://cepr.net/blogs/cepr-blog/scott-walker-foxconn-and-the-wisconsin-economic-development-corporation

ccxxxviii https://www.citylab.com/life/2018/05/what-did-cities-actually-offer-amazon/559220/

ccxxxix https://www.yellowstonepark.com/things-to-do/wolf-reintroduction-changes-ecosystem

ccxl Ripple, William J.; Beschta, Robert L. (2004). "Wolves and the Ecology of Fear: Can Predation Risk Structure Ecosystems?" *BioScience*. Oxford University Press. 54 (8): 755.

ccxli https://us.whales.org/wdc-in-action/climate-change

ccxlii https://www.youtube.com/watch?v=M18HxXve3CM

ccxliii *Williams, J.D.; G. K. Meffe (1998). "Non indigenous Species". Status and Trends of the Nation's Biological Resources. Reston, Virginia: United States Department of the Interior, Geological Survey*

ccxliv https://www.businessinsider.com/tesla-workers-describe-working-in-gigafactory-2018-8

ccxlv https://retail.emarketer.com/article/nearly-half-of-us-households-now-amazon-prime-subscribers/5a72304cebd40008bc791227

ccxlvi

https://www.freep.com/story/entertainment/arts/2018/02/09/ponyride-corktown-move-detroit-make-art-work-recycle-here/321501002/

ccxlvii

https://www.detroitnews.com/story/business/2019/02/19/ponyrid
e-small-business-incubator-sells-corktown-building/2915785002/
ccxlviii https://floridapolitics.com/archives/295317-st-pete-launches-
partnership-with-entrepreneurs-to-enhance-city-efficiency
ccxlix For the Love of Cities, citation
ccl http://www.cityoforlando.net/flag/

Peter Kageyama

APPENDIX